DEHYDRATOR COOKBOOK
FOR BEGINNERS

Dehydrator Cookbook

for Beginners

A Guide to Dehydrating Fruits, Vegetables, Meats, and More

Chris Dalziel

ROCKRIDGE
PRESS

*To Sarah, Ian, and Christopher,
who inspire me to choose joy and
preserve it, each and every day.*

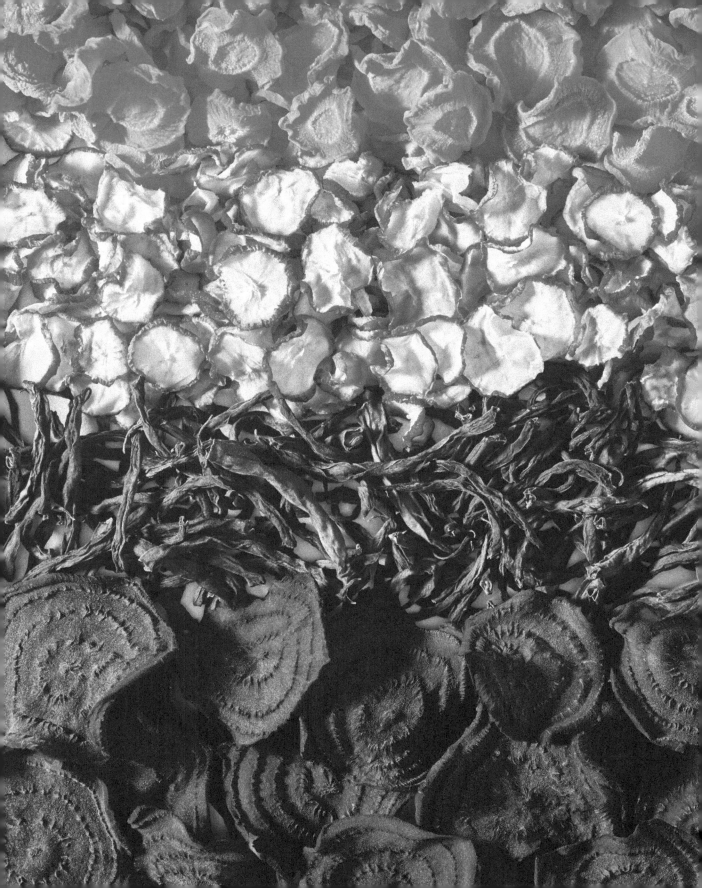

CONTENTS

INTRODUCTION

Did you know that dehydrating is one of the oldest and easiest methods of food preservation? It's also one of the most versatile methods. With a dehydrator, you can preserve fruits, vegetables, meat, and seafood. You can also make healthy and nutritious snacks and even complete meals. Dehydrated foods are portable and keep without refrigeration, making them ideal for lunch boxes, hiking, travel, and long-term food storage.

I started my journey with dehydrating more than 40 years ago, when we purchased our first home, which included mature fruit trees. My dehydrator let me preserve the pears, apples, plums, cherries, and garden bounty easily, saving money and preventing the food from being wasted. Using my dehydrator, I made nutritious treats, such as fruit leather and energy bars for lunches and after-school snacks. Dried apple chips and "pear candy" were a hit at school parties and provided a healthy alternative to potato chips. Dehydrating also saved me time, because each batch of dehydrated food yielded enough for several meals or snacks.

The health benefits of dehydrating are undeniable; this method retains up to 90 percent of the vitamins, minerals, and antioxidants in food. Preserving food by freezing retains about the same nutrition as dehydrating, but frozen food has a shorter shelf life. Dehydrated food is nutritionally superior to canned food; the high temperatures of the canning process deplete vitamin C, vitamin A, and many of the B vitamins.

Dehydrating allows you to control the ingredients in your food. You can choose how much sugar to put in the fruit leather or how much salt to put in your beef jerky. I especially like that you can also control cross-contamination with such common allergens as wheat, peanuts, or soy.

Drying food allows me to be creative both when preserving and using the ingredients in meals and snacks. It also bolsters my confidence, knowing my family is prepared for emergencies with safely stored healthy food, even if the power goes out.

This book is divided into three parts. In the first section, you'll find the basics to help you get started, even if you've never used a dehydrator. You'll learn about the equipment you need, some important techniques to ensure that your food is safe and free of bad bacteria, and how to pretreat food to ensure that the nutrients, texture, flavor, and color are preserved both in drying and in storage.

In part 2, you'll learn how to dry 70 basic ingredients, including fruit, vegetables, meat, poultry, fish, herbs, and spices. You'll probably find that this is the section you refer back to most often.

In part 3, you'll discover how to make your own dehydrated snacks and meals. Snacks are easy to make in the dehydrator and are healthier than store-bought options like veggie chips or fruit leather. When you're looking for nutritious lunch box treats or after-school snacks, you can turn to this section for inspiration. Meals that use dehydrated ingredients and meals that you can prepare for dehydrating are both included. You can use these meals for lunch on the go, camping, emergency preparedness—or even for family dinner!

The food-drying recipes in this book are for use with an electric dehydrator. No alternatives are given for oven drying or solar drying. But with the easy-to-navigate directions, you'll be using your electric dehydrator with confidence in no time!

Inside, you'll also find Dehydrating Quick Tips that include important information, time-savers, and pro tips to help you make the most of your dehydrator.

PART I

All about Dehydrating

Dehydrating is a simple way to preserve food. Your dehydrator allows you to create healthy, nutritious pantry items, spices, snacks, and even complete meals that can be safely stored at room temperature for many months. Your dehydrator makes the job easier and faster by controlling the variables of temperature and humidity. Dehydrating helps you reduce food waste, stock your pantry, try new snack ideas, make food for road trips and camping, and create meals that align with your personal values and dietary needs.

Dehydrated food retains many of the nutrients of fresh food far better than other methods of food preservation. Fresh food can lose up to 50 percent of its nutritional value sitting in the refrigerator. But dried food retains all the antioxidants and minerals of fresh food, and most of the vitamins. Dehydrated food weighs less and takes up less space in the pantry, making it ideal for road trips, hiking, emergency preparedness, and weekday meal prep. Let's dive in!

CHAPTER 1

Dehydrating Basics

Before you start making yummy fruit leather, apple slices, and beet chips, we'll need to cover a few basics. Dehydrating is a fun and creative way to preserve food and make nutritious snacks and meals, but there are a few things that don't dehydrate well or should be avoided.

There are many reasons to dehydrate, and while you might have a main motivation, some of these other reasons might also resonate with you. Knowing beforehand what goals you have in dehydrating can help you make the best use of your investment of time and money.

Dehydrated food has the same nutritional value as fresh food, but how the food is handled during preparation for dehydrating, as well as the care taken in preparing the finished food for storage, can impact the safety and nutrition of your finished food.

The Wonder of Dehydrating

A centuries-old technology, dehydrating removes moisture from fresh food so bacteria cannot grow. Dehydrating preserves your food for a year or more, without refrigeration. With 90 percent of the moisture removed, the food intensifies in flavor, concentrates its nutritional value, and takes up less room in your pantry.

In areas where the relative humidity is 30 percent or less, fruit naturally dries on the tree or vine, right in the garden. Airflow and heat are both essential to the dehydrating process. When left to nature, grapes turn into raisins slowly, dependent on local weather conditions. But in many areas the humidity is too high for this natural process to be successful. A food dehydrator controls the variables of temperature and humidity, speeding up the drying process and ensuring an end product that is safely preserved.

The first food-drying machine was invented in France in 1795 to aid Napoleon's war efforts. It used circulating airflow and temperature control to speed up the dehydration process. Dried food was useful for traveling armies because it was lightweight, retained its nutritional value, and took up less space than its fresh counterpart.

During the two world wars, dehydrated food was essential to provisioning the troops, leading to an increased demand and further innovation on an industrial scale. In fact, instant mashed potatoes were born from the war effort with the technology gained from dehydrating food for the troops.

Interest in home dehydrating was slower to take hold until the mid 1970s, when the back-to-the-land movement increased interest in home-scale food preservation. In response to this increased demand, several electric dehydrators for home use were patented that offered both airflow and heat.

Dehydrators for home use offer continuous circulating airflow, temperature control, food-safe tray materials, and special aftermarket add-ons like silicone sheets to make it easier to make leathers and snacks. The latest digital models allow for temperature control between sections of the dehydrator, as well as programmable temperature and time variations for different foods. With electronic precision, you can put the food in, set the cycle, and go about your day.

What Should (and Shouldn't) Be Dehydrated

Fruits and vegetables are the easiest and most forgiving foods to process. Dried fruit can be eaten without rehydrating. It's a nutrient-dense food that makes an ideal snack. It can be added to oatmeal, muffins, and hot cereal to improve the nutritional quality of simple meals.

Dried vegetables are convenient for soups, stews, sauces, and dips where they can be rehydrated in the cooking process. Aromatic vegetables such as onions, garlic, carrots, celery, and peppers can be used as ingredients in meals on their own or combined into spice blends to add flavor to other dishes.

Lean meat, poultry, and fish can also be dehydrated, provided a few precautions are taken with these high-protein foods. When dehydrating, temperatures should reach 165°F (74°C) to kill any spoilage organisms. If your dehydrator doesn't go this high, place the food in the dehydrator at 145°F for at least 4 hours, until it is done. Then put it in a preheated oven at 275°F for 10 minutes so that it reaches an internal temperature of 165°F (74°C).

Cured ham can be successfully dehydrated, but pork should never be dehydrated at home or used for jerky. The temperatures used in a home dehydrator cannot destroy the trichinella parasite nor other harmful bacteria that are commonly found in pork.

Raw eggs and milk products do not dehydrate well. They are prone to bacterial contamination at dehydrating temperatures.

Fatty and oily foods cannot be dried adequately in a home dehydrator. The fat won't dry properly and as a result, the food spoils quickly. This includes high-fat foods such as avocados and olives.

When dehydrating meat, you should remove all visible fat. Only lean meat, poultry, or fish should be used for dehydrating. Ground meat should be no more than 10 percent fat. Fish like salmon and mackerel have too high a fat content to make them good candidates for dehydrating; they can be dried for short-term storage, but they should not be used for long-term storage due to the increased risk of spoilage.

Foods high in sugar or alcohol won't dry properly. Foods like alcohol-soaked fruit, honey, or candy tend to absorb moisture from the air and resist dehydration.

Benefits of Dehydrating

Everyone comes to dehydrating for different reasons. Some like the convenience and portability of dried food. Others use their dehydrator to preserve their garden veggies. Still others use their dehydrator to make food for hiking or camping trips. I use my dehydrator to preserve produce in season, when it is at the peak of freshness and nutrition. But regardless of your reason for dehydrating food, there are several benefits to dehydrating food that are universal.

Reduction of Spoilage

Dehydrating helps reduce unnecessary food waste. You can stop putting leftovers in the refrigerator and then tossing them in the garbage or compost pile a week or two later when they grow green fuzz. Both leftover vegetables and main dishes can be dehydrated, preserving your investment in healthy food, plus you'll have future meals for busy days. Dehydrating also allows you to stock up on produce discounts like overripe bananas or onions past their prime. Many grocery stores and produce stands have discount bins where "seconds," like citrus fruit, apples, sweet peppers, and tomatoes are offered at significant savings. Dehydrating these foods helps you stock your pantry while saving money.

A church in my community collects excess produce from local grocery stores, dehydrates it, and turns it into dried soup mixes and dried fruit for food banks in several nearby towns. Using a commercial dehydrator with 20 trays, they divert 9,000 pounds of produce from the local landfill each month and convert it into nourishing food for hundreds of families.

Dehydrating also allows you to take advantage of excess produce, whether from your garden or from local farms, while it's in season and at its peak of nutrition. Rather than letting the kale wilt or the zucchini get huge and unpalatable, you can harvest them in their prime, dry them, and stock your pantry.

More Control over Food Contents

When you prepare your snacks and staple foods at home using your dehydrator, you control every step of the process—especially the ingredients. Healthy snack foods that are low in sugar and salt, or food without allergens, can be made easily in your dehydrator. You can adapt recipes to ensure there is no cross-contamination of food, making dehydrating ideal for families who deal with food allergies.

One member of my family has a serious wheat allergy. Almost all commercially dried or freeze-dried food has an ingredient warning "may contain wheat." But by drying our own produce and using our dehydrator for snacks and travel food, I have confidence that the food he eats is safe from cross-contamination, even when we are away from home.

Peanut, soy, milk, wheat, and other common allergens are easier to exclude when you provision your pantry with ingredients that you dehydrate yourself. When you make your own meals and snacks from scratch, you'll no longer need a magnifying glass to read ingredient labels!

You can also control the amount of sugar, starch, artificial colors and flavoring, and other chemical additives when you dry your own food at home. If you have dietary restrictions or preferences, using your dehydrator to make meals or pantry items can help you reach your personal goals.

Raw foodies can control the temperature at which the food is dried, ensuring high availability of enzymes, vitamins, and minerals for their special dietary needs.

Time, Space & Savings

Investing in a dehydrator ultimately saves you money. Buying produce in bulk—and in season—offers considerable savings over grocery-store prices. Fruit, vegetables, and nuts can be purchased in bulk directly from local farms, and then dehydrated while at their peak of flavor and nutrition, at significant savings over buying fresh or even frozen vegetables.

Last fall, I picked up a 20-pound bag of Walla Walla onions for $20 and a 25-pound bag of sweet peppers for $10 from the bargain bin at a farm stand. Walla Walla onions are $3 per pound at my grocery store, and sweet peppers are $4 to $5 per pound. That's a savings of almost $200! In just a few days, I dried all the onions in my dehydrator. I divided the peppers by color and dried the red ones first while waiting for the green ones to ripen.

The dried onions and peppers took up significantly less space in my pantry than the big bags of onions and peppers I brought home. Those two huge bags were reduced to four 1-quart jars and a pint jar that are much easier to store in my modest pantry.

Filling your dehydrator takes a little time, but it saves you time in the long run. Your dehydrated foods become convenience items once they are stored in jars in your pantry. It's so much faster to grab dried onions when you need them than to cut up a raw onion while making dinner. Think of the time it takes to prepare food for your dehydrator, and package it when it's done, as an investment in future convenience.

Emergency Preparedness

Dehydrated food is ideal for emergency food storage. Whether you are preparing for a weather event, a period of unemployment, or a natural disaster, having a 30-day supply of nutritious food on hand is wise.

Dehydrating food your family already eats ensures that you have as little disruption as possible in a real emergency. By stocking your pantry with dehydrated food that you've prepared from wholesome ingredients, you can be assured that your family's nutritional needs are met, even if you can't get to the grocery store.

Dehydrated food, when properly prepared and packaged for long-term storage, can form the foundation of a robust preparedness plan. Taking the extra step to package your dehydrated food in Mylar bags or glass jars with oxygen absorbers ensures that your dehydrated food will still be fresh and retain its nutrients in storage.

But even minor disruptions can be helped by having the convenience of dehydrated food in your pantry. An extra dinner guest, sickness in the house, or an unexpected bill doesn't have to shake your confidence. Having dehydrated ingredients to make your favorite comfort foods already in your pantry can help you move through even minor inconveniences with grace.

High Nutritional Value

When food is dehydrated, the water is removed, but the nutrition in the food remains stable. The flavor and nutrients become more concentrated, and the caloric value remains the same. Dehydrated food has the same calories, protein, fiber, and carbohydrates as fresh food. It also retains the same minerals, fatty acids, and antioxidants as fresh food, as well as most of the vitamins. Dehydrated food retains many of these nutrients in storage, even over several months and years.

There is some loss of vitamin C and some B vitamins during blanching, because some of these water-soluble vitamins are lost in the blanching water. Vegetables that are blanched before dehydrating have the same vitamins as frozen food, but dehydrated food has a longer shelf life. This vitamin loss can be minimized by blanching with steam before dehydrating, rather than immersing vegetables in boiling water prior to dehydrating.

Hikers and athletes benefit from the concentration of nutrients provided by dehydrated foods, allowing them to eat less while maintaining their energy levels.

To ensure that your dehydrated food retains the most nutrition, it should be dehydrated at its peak of ripeness, when the flavor, color, and texture are best. Vegetables that are past their prime and are fading in color, scent, or flavor will not make quality dried vegetables.

Bulk Buying Food for Dehydrating

Save money by purchasing food in bulk when it is in season and dehydrating it for later. This is when the food is the most flavorful and nutritious. Visit local you-pick farms or orchards and buy fruit and vegetables by the case, direct from the grower, to get the most value for your money.

However, as you make your buying decisions, keep in mind how much produce you can realistically get through your dehydrator. Most dehydrators with at least 8 square feet of drying area can dry 25 pounds of fruit or vegetables in a day.

Apples purchased in bulk can reasonably last a month or more to allow you time for processing. Pears need to be dehydrated within a week if they are still green, or immediately if they have already turned yellow. Vegetables with a natural waxy coating, like peppers, last longer than tomatoes at room temperature. Plan to process fully ripe tomatoes within a few days of purchase.

Skip over the fading-green kale in the refrigerator vegetable bin. Choose the most vibrant-colored vegetables to get the most nutrition from your dehydrated food.

High in Flavor (and Deliciousness)

Dehydrated fruit tastes like candy. The sugar in the fruit is concentrated along with the flavor. During the dehydration process, some of the sugars in fruit caramelize, giving the fruit a rich, buttery flavor that is more than just concentrated fruit juice.

Surprisingly, many dehydrated vegetables also get a richer, sweeter flavor when dehydrated. Carrots, beets, parsnips, sweet potatoes, and winter squash concentrate their sugars during dehydration, making them equally at home in a dessert-like fruit leather or a vegetable soup.

Herbs and spices also concentrate their flavors during dehydration as the water evaporates and the volatile oils are concentrated in the plant cells. Onions have a richer onion fragrance and flavor that is sweeter and more subtle than raw onions. Basil completely changes its flavor after dehydration, losing the anise note that is prevalent in fresh basil, allowing the minty camphor flavor to predominate.

Dehydrated food is more nutrient-dense and highly flavored, so a little goes a long way. One quarter cup of onion flakes is the equivalent of one onion, and ½ cup of most dried vegetables is the equivalent of 1 cup of fresh. Just over 1 pound of dried tomatoes is the equivalent of 20 pounds of fresh tomatoes, and 1 tablespoon of tomato powder is the equivalent of ½ cup of tomato sauce.

Addressing Safety Concerns

Dehydrating food is easy and fun, but there are a few safety concerns to keep in mind when preparing food for long-term storage. Dehydrating removes moisture from food and slows down the growth of bacteria, but it doesn't kill pathogens that are already on the food.

It's important to minimize bacterial contamination of the food at every step of the food-preservation process. Before you begin, clean all surfaces or utensils that will touch your food with a mild all-purpose cleaning solution. Your dehydrator and trays should be clean with no visible food debris, to prevent off-flavors and bacterial contamination. Clean your dehydrator and trays after every batch to minimize the chance for spoilage organisms to grow.

Only dehydrate food that is clean and free of mold or rot. If you see any mold on your food, discard all the food that had contact with it, even if there was no visible mold on it. Mold spores can contaminate your dehydrator and all the food in the dehydrator, making the food unsafe for consumption.

DEHYDRATION QUICK TIP
Produce Wash

Washing produce before dehydrating removes bacteria, dirt, and some pesticides. This wash was found to remove 97 percent of contaminants.

◆ **3 cups cold water**

◆ **1 cup distilled white vinegar**

◆ **½ teaspoon liquid castile soap or detergent**

Allow the produce to soak in the mixture for 3 to 5 minutes. The soap won't harm the food, but helps dissolve pesticide residues. Rinse thoroughly. Pat the food with a towel to dry before processing fruit or vegetables for dehydrating.

Wash your hands before preparing food for the dehydrator, before touching food inside the dehydrator, and before packaging food for storage, to prevent bacterial contamination. Your hands must be completely dry before packaging dehydrated food so that you don't introduce moisture to the food, which can encourage mold or bacteria to grow in the sealed packaging.

When working with raw meat, fish, or poultry, clean all surfaces before and after with a mild disinfectant to prevent the contamination of other food with the raw meat. To prevent cross-contamination, use a dedicated cutting board for raw meat that you don't use for other food.

To ensure that your dehydrated food is safe and will have an extended shelf life, follow the steps in each recipe for food preparation, specific temperatures, time guidelines, and storage best practices. Dehydrated food that is properly prepared, dehydrated, and stored in glass jars or Mylar bags will have an extended shelf life that surpasses most other food-preservation methods.

Uses for Dehydrated Food

Dehydrated food is a versatile addition to your kitchen. With a pantry full of dehydrated ingredients, you'll be able to put together menu items easily and creatively. Many of the recipes in this book will become essential ingredients in your cooking. What would winter soup be without carrots, onions, and celery? Your salsa is almost finished with dried hot peppers, tomato powder, dried onions, garlic, and limes.

You'll find recipes for many of the following staples in this book.

Marinades, Sauces & Teas

Aromatic vegetables such as onions, peppers, garlic, herbs, and spices provide the ingredients for marinades, sauces, and meat rubs. Whether you like your sauces spicy or mild, you can control the heat by choosing the chilies ahead of time and drying the ones with the heat level that you prefer.

These same aromatic vegetables are the basis for vegetable soup, sauces, and spice blends. Many herbs can be dried in your dehydrator and then used for herbal tea. Lemon balm, mint, and rose hips make a relaxing blend that's ideal at the end of a busy day. Thyme, sage, and oregano make a throat-soothing tea for winter dryness. Whether your goal for tea is happy feelings or health, your dehydrated herbs can help you create the best tea blends for your needs.

Stand-Alones or Additions

Dehydrated fruits and vegetables can be used as stand-alone ingredients as well. Eat them plain as snacks or add them to cereal or oatmeal. Granola is a combination of oatmeal and dried fruits and nuts. It is easy to make from your dehydrated fruit.

Using special techniques, you can turn fresh vegetables into healthy chips for snacking. Beet chips are my personal favorite, but you can also make chips from other root vegetables, including sweet potatoes.

Dried fruit can be eaten as a snack without rehydrating. Dried fruit "candy" is an indispensable treat at my house when my granddaughters visit, and healthier than cookies. At the last visit, one of them put in an order for "apple candy" for her lunch box.

Fruit leather is a versatile way to add dried fruit to your menu. They can be made of a single fruit like apples (see recipe on page 124), or a combination of fruit like strawberries and rhubarb, or peaches and apples.

Dried vegetables are usually rehydrated to prepare them for serving as a side, but I also like to use them as a healthy addition to fruit leather. Pumpkin Spice Latte Leather (page 131) is a fun seasonal treat to make in the fall.

Soups & Meals

Dehydrated food can also be the main part of your meal planning, offering convenience and economy for a weeknight menu. Add water or chicken stock to the Vegetable Soup Blend (page 145) for a soup served with bread for a quick dinner. Or use it as the basis for a more substantial soup or stew like Butternut Squash Soup (page 137), Shepherd's Pie (page 150), or Hamburger Stew (page 149).

In chapter 8, you'll find recipes that use your dehydrated ingredients as the main ingredients to help you get your meals on the table fast, such as Fajita Chicken (page 146) and Potatoes O'Brien (page 152). You'll also find meals to make and dehydrate to supplement your pantry with ready-made conveniences such as Black Bean Chili (page 136), Coconut Shrimp & Rice Curry (page 140), and Curry Chicken with Rice (page 142).

Your dehydrator can be a year-round asset to your kitchen, enabling you to stock your pantry and put healthy, nutritious meals on your table quickly and conveniently.

CHAPTER 2

Before You Dehydrate

While dehydrating is easy to master, there are subtleties and strategies that can make your dehydrated food taste even better. In this chapter, you'll learn about the different types of dehydrators and how they work to reduce the moisture content in food for long-term preservation. You'll get a rundown of kitchen tools needed to make the work of dehydrating easier. You'll be introduced to several pretreatments that can preserve the texture, color, flavor, and nutrients in your dehydrated food. You'll also discover the best ways to store your dehydrated food for long-term food security. Finally, you'll be given ways to rehydrate your dried food so you can use it in meal planning.

Understanding Your Equipment

Your dehydrator is a precision-engineered appliance that is designed to remove moisture from food in a controlled way that preserves nutrients in food. There are two main types of dehydrators, but both use continuous airflow and heat to get the job done. This section will help you get to know your own dehydrator well so you can get the maximum benefit from this tool. You'll learn how a dehydrator works to dry fresh food, but it's always important to consult the instruction manual that come with your own dehydrator.

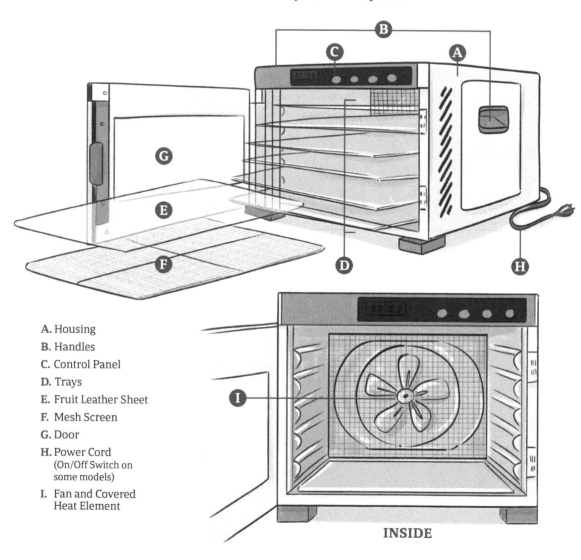

A. Housing

B. Handles

C. Control Panel

D. Trays

E. Fruit Leather Sheet

F. Mesh Screen

G. Door

H. Power Cord
(On/Off Switch on some models)

I. Fan and Covered Heat Element

INSIDE

Getting to Know Your Dehydrator

There are two main types of dehydrators available. Tabletop dehydrators usually cost less than $100. Cabinet-style dehydrators cost more, starting at $150 and going up to as much as $1,000. But regardless of design, both types contain five main components:

◆ A motor

◆ A heat source

◆ A fan to circulate warm air over the food

◆ A rack to hold trays equal distance apart to allow for airflow

◆ Trays with mesh screens to hold the food

Tabletop dehydrators with stacking trays have the motor, heat source, and fan on either the top or bottom of the unit. The warm air is forced vertically through the food in the trays. With these appliances, the trays that are farthest away from the heat source receive less warmth than the trays closest to the heat source. In these models, trays need to be rotated during the drying process to ensure that all food dries evenly.

Dehydrators with a bottom-mounted motor may end up with drippings falling into the motor housing. With these models, you'll want to keep the motor clean and free of debris to prevent premature failure of the motor. Dehydrators with top-mounted motors avoid this problem.

Cabinet-style dehydrators have the fan and heat source in the back of the unit. The fans blow the warmed air horizontally over and under the food on the trays, allowing for even drying of all trays. The food near the back of the tray, closest to the motor, receives more warmth than the food at the front of the trays near the door of the dehydrator. Rotating the trays 180 degrees halfway through the drying time allows the food to dry evenly.

Tabletop dehydrators are great for occasional use, making snacks, dehydrating left-overs, or drying herbs. However, cabinet-style dehydrators are more efficient, with superior temperature control. If you plan to dry a lot of produce at one time or make jerky regularly, you'll be happier with a cabinet-style dehydrator.

How It Works

Your dehydrator is designed to efficiently evaporate moisture from food using warm air. Vents placed near the fan draw room air into the dehydrator chamber. The heating element warms this air inside the chamber. The fan circulates warmed air through the food, removing moisture and carrying it out of the dehydrator via carefully placed vents on the opposite side. Cabinet-style dehydrators have doors that fit loosely, allowing moist, circulating air to escape. This is done intentionally and is not a defect.

The food trays inside your dehydrator have a grid pattern of holes to allow the air to fully circulate through the food, speeding up the drying time. Some dehydrators have additional silicone or plastic sheets to use for liquids or purees, preventing the food from leaking down over the food below. When these sheets are used, drying times may be longer, because airflow is impeded.

Simple dehydrators have only an on/off switch, but more sophisticated units have a temperature control dial that allows you to select the temperature for different kinds of food. Herbs can be dried at the lowest temperature to preserve their flavor, and meat can be dried safely at higher temperatures.

Cleaning & Maintenance

Your dehydrator should be cleaned after every batch to minimize bacterial contamination and keep the unit clean and operating at full efficiency. If you won't be using your dehydrator for a while, put it away in its original box after cleaning and letting it dry thoroughly. Clean it again, following these steps, before its next use.

◆ Remove the trays and any tray liners used during a dehydrating batch.

◆ Place both trays and tray liners in a sink with hot, soapy water. Soak to remove any stuck-on food. Wash with a soft bristle brush or sponge. Rinse in clear water and towel dry.

◆ While the dehydrator is empty, wipe down the inside of the dehydrator with a mild detergent. Remove any debris. Pay attention to the tray holders and the fan covers, as food can get stuck on them.

◆ Wipe down the doors on both sides and dry with a soft towel. Avoid using abrasive cleansers on the door so you don't scratch the door material.

◆ Replace the trays.

◆ Periodically test the temperature setting with an empty dehydrator by placing a meat thermometer on an empty tray. Run the dehydrator for 60 minutes. Check the temperature on the thermometer. If it reads less than you expected, check your owner's manual to troubleshoot the issue.

Other Essential Tools & Equipment

There are a few other tools that I find indispensable when I am prepping food for dehydrating or storage. These are time-saving tools that make the job faster and easier:

Sharp vegetable knife or chef's knife—A reliable knife will carry some weight and hold a sharp edge for many cuts. The sharper the knife, the less stress on your wrist and the less likely you will cut yourself in the kitchen.

Mandoline—This is a tool that cuts thin, uniform slices and makes cutting onions, cucumbers, beets, and other vegetables easy and fast. The right mandoline should have both an adjustable blade and a hand guard to protect your fingers.

Jerky gun—If you plan to make a lot of jerky from ground meat, a jerky gun can save you time.

Dishwasher-safe cutting board—These are essential for preparing jerky and raw meat. A dedicated cutting board should be reserved for meat and not be used for the preparation of vegetables and fruit.

Prep bowls—At least three prep bowls in two sizes can make pretreatments easier. I use two 1-quart stainless-steel bowls and one 3-quart stainless-steel bowl. These are also useful for marinating jerky.

Blender—A high-powered blender makes it easy to puree fruit for fruit leather and powder dried vegetables and herbs. Choose one with at least 1,400 watts of power.

A steam basket or colander—Choose one that fits inside a stovetop saucepan for blanching.

A slotted spoon—Use for removing pieces of fruit after pretreatment.

Plastic mesh sheets—Most dehydrators come with plastic mesh sheets, but stainless-steel dehydrators might only have wire trays.

Fruit leather sheets, parchment paper, or plastic wrap—These help keep liquids from leaking through the food tray holes.

Don't Let the Food Fall on the Floor

As food is dehydrated, it shrinks on the trays, taking up much less space than the original raw food. The trays in some dehydrators have grids with large holes that allow the finished dehydrated food to fall through. It can be frustrating after washing, slicing, and drying to have the finished food fall on the floor just as you take the tray from the dehydrator. Aftermarket tray material is available to solve this frustration.

The tray material is sold in rolls that can be cut to size to fit any dehydrator. The heat from the dehydrator flattens the plastic permanently, allowing the tray material to take the shape of the tray frames it is placed in.

If you've had the frustration of your dehydrated food falling through your dehydrator tray holes as it shrinks, check the Resources section (page 158) for the suppliers of these aftermarket tray materials.

Pretreating

Some fruits and vegetables turn brown when exposed to oxygen. This oxidation can be minimized by using pretreatments that either seal the surface of the fruit, preventing oxidation, or introduce an antioxidant like vitamin C to counteract oxidation. Furthermore, some vegetables require blanching to stop enzymatic action that can reduce nutrients and give your food off-flavors. Not all foods require pretreatment, though. The recipes in this book note if pretreatment is necessary or recommended as well as which pretreatments to use.

Blanching

Blanching stops the enzymes that turn sugars into starch in vegetables or continue the ripening process to the point of rot. It improves the appearance, texture, and flavor of many dehydrated foods. In general, foods that are normally eaten raw, such as peppers or tomatoes, do not need blanching. Foods that are eaten cooked, such as corn, beans, or peas, can benefit from blanching.

There are several ways to blanch produce before dehydrating.

STEAM BLANCHING

Steam blanching is the method I use most often. It preserves the most nutrients because the vegetables don't sit in water (fruit doesn't require blanching). To do this, place a steam basket on top of a pot of boiling water and cover it to hold in the steam. Place the prepared vegetables in the basket and steam for only 1 to 2 minutes. Rinse the hot vegetables with cold water to stop the cooking process, then drain before dehydrating.

WATER BLANCHING

With water blanching, you place the vegetables directly in boiling water and boil for the required time for each vegetable. Then vegetables are removed using a slotted spoon or tongs, and chilled in ice water.

With this method, about half the vitamin C and some B vitamins are lost to the blanching water. All other nutrients remain stable.

DEHYDRATION QUICK TIP

Conditioning Dehydrated Food

When food appears to be fully dry, it may still have some trapped moisture inside the cells. Conditioning evens out the moisture level in dried food so that food that is almost dry can complete the drying process. This is especially important in moist fruits like pears, apricots, strawberries, and plums.

To condition food, allow it to cool completely. Place the food in a large bowl or jar. Cover with an airtight lid to exclude humid air. Stir the food in the bowl or shake the jar to distribute the food. Look for signs of moisture such as condensation on the side of the glass jar. If you see condensation, return the food to the dehydrator and dry it for a few more hours. After a few days, you can safely put the dehydrated food into a permanent storage container.

Food stored in Mason jars can be easily checked for condensation. Simply turn the jars upside down. Condensation forms on the bottom of the jar and on the sides if there is residual moisture in the food.

SYRUP BLANCHING

Syrup blanching is used to pretreat some fruit, such as figs, apples, pears, and plums, when the fruit is used for desserts. Make a simple syrup for blanching by adding 2 cups of corn syrup and 2 cups of sugar to 4 cups of water. The corn syrup prevents the sugar from crystalizing on the fruit during dehydrating. Heat the syrup and add the fruit. Simmer the fruit for 8 to 10 minutes. Turn off the heat and leave the fruit in the syrup for an additional 20 minutes. Remove the fruit from the syrup. Dehydrate as usual.

Acid, Honey & Assorted Treatments

Heat blanching is normally used with vegetables, but there are alternatives to blanching fruit to prevent oxidation and browning.

ASCORBIC ACID DIP

For fruit that is prone to oxidation, such as pears and peaches, my favorite pretreatment is ascorbic acid or vitamin C. Of all the options, it is the most effective at preventing browning. Ascorbic acid powder can be found in most drugstores where vitamins are sold. In a prep bowl, dissolve 1 tablespoon of vitamin C powder (9,000 mg) in 1 quart of cold water. Place the prepared fruit in the solution and let it sit for a minute. Remove the fruit with a slotted spoon. Drain the fruit and place it on the dehydrator trays.

CITRIC ACID DIP

Like ascorbic acid, citric acid acidifies the water, thus preventing oxidation. Use 1 tablespoon of citric acid per quart of water. Citric acid can give fruit a sour taste. Place the prepared fruit in the solution. Allow the fruit to sit for 1 minute and remove it with a slotted spoon. Place it on the dehydrator trays once the fruit has drained.

COMMERCIAL FRUIT DIP

You can find antioxidant treatments, such as Ball® Fruit-Fresh, in the produce section or the canning section of the grocery store. They contain a combination of ascorbic acid and citric acid, along with other ingredients. Use these according to the directions on the package. Commercial fruit dips are convenient to use and may be easier to find than ascorbic acid powder or citric acid; however, they contain anticaking agents and sugar.

HONEY DIP

Honey adds additional sweetness to fruit that's been pretreated with it. Honey prevents browning by sealing the surface of the fruit, preventing oxidation. To make a honey dip, add 1 cup of sugar and 1 cup of honey to 3 cups of slightly warm water. Dip fruit a few pieces at a time in the honey dip. Drain fully before dehydrating.

FRUIT JUICE SOAK

Lemon, lime, or pineapple juice can be used as an antioxidant dip. Both lemon and lime juice contain ascorbic acid and citric acid. In a prep bowl, add 1 cup of fruit juice to 4 cups of warm water, place the prepared fruit in the bowl and let it soak for no more than 10 minutes. Remove it with a slotted spoon and allow it to drain completely before dehydrating.

Recognizing Doneness

Food is done when it is dry enough to prevent bacteria from growing and spoiling the food. Different foods have different moisture requirements for safe food storage. The amount of moisture left in dehydrated food affects its flexibility. The more moisture, the more flexible your dehydrated food will be. You'll find specific guidelines in each produce entry and in each recipe to test for doneness so you won't be guessing. But here are some general guidelines for vegetables, fruit, herbs, and meat to get you started.

◆ Allow a sample to cool completely before testing for doneness. Most dehydrated food is flexible when warm but will firm up when cooled. If you are in doubt, dehydrate the food for a few more hours. It's better to dry longer than to stop drying too soon.

◆ Vegetables are usually done when they are leathery and brittle. When pressed between the thumb and forefinger, they should snap cleanly in half, without bending.

◆ Fruit is done when it is leathery but still flexible, and no soft pockets remain in the fruit. If you find soft, squishy sections, give the fruit more time. When the fruit is done, there will be no soft spots.

◆ Herbs are done when the leaves crumble when crushed. Stems should be hard and brittle. If the stems bend, they need more time.

◆ Meat should be dry and leathery with little flexibility when done, but specific meats vary in the test for doneness.

Storage

Once your food is properly dehydrated, your job isn't finished. It's important to package the food and store it to protect it from spoilage. Moisture, oxygen, and light can degrade your stored food, shortening the shelf life and allowing bacteria to ruin the food.

When stored properly and protected from moisture, heat, and light, dehydrated food can last for up to 10 years. The actual shelf life varies depending on the food, with fruit lasting longer than vegetables because the natural sugar in fruit helps extend its shelf life. (Consult the recipes for specifics on storage needs and the shelf life of individual foods.)

If you see any signs of spoilage, such as off-odors or mold, discard the contents of the package. It is not safe to eat.

Key Equipment

There are a few pieces of equipment that can make storing your dehydrated food easier and more successful.

STORAGE CONTAINERS

The best choice for long-term storage are glass canning jars and lids, or Mylar bags of at least 7 ml thickness (thinner Mylar bags can be pierced by the sharp edges of dried vegetables). When you open the container, you will introduce oxygen and moisture, shortening the food's storage window. So, choose a container size that fits food you can eat in a week or two.

OXYGEN ABSORBERS

Removing oxygen from the storage container extends the shelf life of stored food. This can be achieved by using oxygen absorbers inside the closed container (see the Dehydration Quick Tip on page 26). Oxygen absorbers are small packets of iron dust that react with oxygen, causing the dust to rust. This removes the oxygen from the sealed environment. As oxygen is removed, nitrogen is left in the container. Without oxygen,

insect pests cannot survive and oxidation is halted. Select the oxygen absorber that is sized to the container you are using. Oxygen absorbers are generally used inside sealed Mylar bags to scavenge residual oxygen. It can be beneficial to also use them inside glass jars that are vacuum-sealed, providing an additional layer of protection from spoilage.

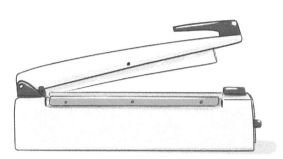

VACUUM SEALERS

Vacuum sealers also remove oxygen from a sealed container. Food sealed in vacuum-sealed bags should be further sealed in a Mylar bag or bucket to prevent oxygen leaks. The hard edges of dehydrated food can pierce the thinner material of vacuum-sealer bags. Mason jars can be vacuum-sealed in a vacuum chamber or with the use of a special jar

---

DEHYDRATION QUICK TIP

Working with Oxygen Absorbers

When choosing an oxygen absorber, use a 200 cc oxygen absorber for a 1-quart jar or a 300 cc oxygen absorber for a ½- to 1-gallon bucket or jar. It is all right to use a larger oxygen absorber than necessary. Oxygen absorbers are single-use items and should not be reused.

Once you open a sealed bag of oxygen absorbers, the clock starts ticking, as they begin to take in oxygen immediately. According to industry standards, you have 30 minutes of air exposure before the oxygen absorbers are done and can no longer absorb additional oxygen. To protect them from oxygen, open the sealed package and place all the oxygen absorbers in a Mason jar with a lid and ring and tightly close.

Place your dehydrated food in Mason jars or Mylar bags. Working quickly, place an appropriate oxygen absorber in each container. Reseal the Mason jar that holds the oxygen absorbers. Then seal each food container either by vacuum sealing (in the case of Mason jars) or with an impulse sealer (see page 27), in the case of Mylar bags.

lid attachment. FoodSaver® makes a vacuum-sealer jar lid accessory that allows you to seal widemouthed and regular-mouth jars with canning lids, removing the air inside the Mason jar. Both handheld vacuum sealers and tabletop vacuum sealers can be used with the jar lid accessory. See the manufacturer's instructions for compatibility before you purchase.

FOOD-GRADE BUCKETS

When storing food in Mylar or vacuum-sealed bags, additional protection from rodent damage is needed for long-term food storage. Plastic buckets provide a barrier from small rodents, although in some areas more protection may be needed. Food stored in vacuum-sealed bags should also be stored in plastic buckets or hard-sided containers to protect them from rodent damage.

SILICA GEL PACKETS

Silica gel packets absorb residual moisture inside the container. They can be helpful if you live in a humid region.

IMPULSE SEALER

When using Mylar bags, an impulse sealer is used to seal the bag opening, after the food and an oxygen absorber are added to the bag. For security, seal the bag three times with the impulse sealer to prevent oxygen leakage through the seal. There is no need to vacuum-seal Mylar bags when an adequate size of oxygen absorber is used.

CANNING JAR FUNNEL

A large-mouthed funnel makes filling jars or Mylar bags easier and tidier by preventing spillage. It is essential for packaging powders but useful for packaging other types of dehydrated food as well.

Storage Techniques

When storing dehydrated food, clean work surfaces and equipment before you begin. With clean hands or wearing gloves, fill the Mason jars or Mylar bags with food, leaving 1 or 2 inches of headspace. Add the appropriate size of oxygen absorber to the container and seal with the appropriate method.

Label bags or jars with a permanent marker, noting the type of food and the date you dehydrated and packaged it. Labels can fall off jars and bags, so I prefer to write this information directly on the Mylar bag or the lid of the jar. Additional information—such as how to rehydrate the dried food or how to use it in a recipe—can be added to a label, placed on the outside of the jar, for convenience.

If you are using Mylar bags, additional protection from rodent and pet damage is necessary. Place the sealed bags inside a 5-gallon food-grade plastic bucket, plastic storage container, or metal can. There is no need to add additional oxygen absorbers to this container if you put oxygen absorbers inside the Mylar bags.

Plastic buckets or containers should not be stored where the container can make direct contact with a cement floor, cement wall, or soil, as moisture can be introduced. Place a carpet or wooden barrier between the cement and the bucket if you are storing food buckets in a basement.

Containers of food should be placed where the ambient temperature is stable. The storage life can be extended by keeping food at temperatures between 50°F and 60°F year-round. A basement storage space is ideal for long-term food storage.

Removing light from the storage area preserves the antioxidants, vitamins, and color of the food. If you don't have a dedicated food-storage space, light can be blocked by placing Mason jars inside paper sleeves or brown bags.

Your home-dehydrated food should be rotated annually. Although it will keep for several years if properly packaged for long-term storage, the nutritional content is best if consumed within a year.

Rehydrating

Rehydrating restores the moisture to dried food, returning it to its original size, form, and appearance. Rehydrated food retains its aroma, flavor, and texture as well as its nutritional content. There are several methods for rehydrating dried food, but in their simplest form, they all add moisture back into the food using either cold or hot liquids.

As a general rule, 1 cup of liquid reconstitutes 1 cup of dehydrated food. If the food hasn't softened enough after an hour, add more liquid. The liquid can be plain water, broth, juice, or milk. Fruit can also be reconstituted in liqueur or brandy.

Most fruit and vegetables reconstitute in one to two hours. However, larger pieces of food may take longer to reconstitute than powders or finely diced pieces. Generally, food that took longer to dehydrate also takes longer to rehydrate. Use only enough liquid as the food will absorb. Using too much liquid makes the food soggy and unappetizing.

Soaking does not take the place of cooking. Food still needs to be cooked after it is reconstituted by soaking.

Save the soaking liquid to add to soups, stews, or cereals. It contains the water-soluble vitamins and minerals leached from the dehydrated food.

Methods

There are two main methods of rehydrating: cold soaking and hot soaking.

Cold soaking should be used for foods that are commonly eaten raw, like fruit. It is a slower process that allows the tissues of the food to relax and absorb the liquid. Food that is reconstituted in room-temperature or cooler water retains its shape and texture better than food rehydrated using hot water.

The soaking liquid, like juice or yogurt, adds additional flavor as it rehydrates the food, but don't add additional salt or sugar to the soaking water, as they hinder the rehydration process. These can be added once the food is fully hydrated.

Use hot soaking when the food being rehydrated will be served cooked or added to a hot dish. Hot soaking breaks some of the plant cells as it rehydrates the food, causing the food to become softer. Hot soaking rehydrates food quicker than cold soaking.

Rehydrating the food while cooking it is fast and easy. Place dried vegetables in soups, stews, or sauces and rehydrate as the sauce cooks on the stovetop. Add dried fruit to sauces, puddings, and warm cereals during the cooking process and rehydrate it while the rest of the mixture cooks.

PART II

Dehydrating
A to Z

Your dehydrator allows you to stock your pantry with wholesome ingredients that are stable at room temperature. Preserved at their peak of freshness and flavor, these ingredients become the resources for future nutritious meals and snacks.

In this section, you'll find 70 ingredients, including common fruits and vegetables, herbs and spices, meat, fish, and poultry. Each ingredient has specific preparation and dehydrating instructions, although times will vary depending on your own ambient temperatures and humidity. Rehydrating suggestions are also included to take the guesswork out of your meal preparations with dehydrated food.

CHAPTER 3

Dehydrating Fruits, Legumes & Nuts

Dried fruits, nuts, and legumes are some of the easiest ingredients to dry. Dried fruit and nuts can be eaten directly from your pantry as healthy snacks without rehydrating, or used in a number of recipes as dry ingredients.

Choose firm, unblemished fruit at the peak of ripeness for the best flavor and texture in your dried fruit. Handle fruit gently to avoid bruising it. Instead of drying it individually, use soft, overripe, or bruised fruit for fruit leather.

Pieces of fruit should be dried until they are firm and leathery but still some-what flexible. Thinner pieces of fruit may dry before thicker pieces. Remove these pieces from the dehydrator as they are done so they don't overdry or darken from burnt sugars.

Pretreat fruit before drying (see page 21) to prevent oxidation and browning. Many of these recipes recommend using ascorbic acid solution (see page 23). If you notice your fruit turning brown in the dehydrator, it indicates that the temperature is too high and the sugars in the fruit are caramelizing, and you'll want to turn down the temperature of your dehydrator. Larger dehydrators can run hotter in the top portion, leading to unwanted browning. Rotating trays partway through the drying cycle can alleviate this.

After drying—but before packaging to store it—condition your fruit (see page 22) to even out the moisture and ensure that stored fruit remains dry and safe to eat. For long-term storage, protect fruit from oxygen degradation by vacuum-sealing it or packaging it with oxygen absorbers (see page 26).

Nuts, seeds, and peanuts contain germination inhibitors that prevent sprouting until the environment is right. These inhibitors may cause digestive upset when the nuts are consumed. Long soaking and then dehydrating at a low temperature removes these inhibitors, making the nuts more digestible and their nutrients more bioavailable. Nuts and seeds should be soaked for 7 to 24 hours to remove these antinutrients. The larger the nut, the longer the soaking time.

Blanch fresh legumes such as peas or chickpeas before drying them to keep them sweet. Without blanching, they become starchy and lose flavor. After blanching, dry them until they are hard and brittle.

Apples

Prep time: 15 minutes / **Dehydration time:** 8 to 12 hours
Yield: 2 to 3 apples = 1 cup dried = 1½ cups rehydrated

Dried apples are delicious, healthy snacks. For the best flavor, choose fully ripe, firm, unblemished apples, with tight skin. Firm apples like Golden Delicious, Gala, Fuji, and Honeycrisp are the best for dehydrating, although you can use any kind of apple you have on hand.

To Prepare

1. Wash the apples in cold water with a squirt of dish soap and vinegar. Soak them briefly to remove grime and pesticide residues, then rinse and dry.

2. Peeling the apples is optional (much of the nutrition in apples is close to the peel). Core the apples and cut them into ¼-inch slices.

3. Soak the slices in ascorbic acid solution for 1 minute, then drain them.

4. Arrange the slices in a single layer on the dehydrator trays.

To Dehydrate

1. Dehydrate at 135°F for 4 hours. Reduce the temperature to 125°F and continue drying for 4 to 8 hours.

2. When dried, the apples should be leathery and crisp, with no spongy areas in the middle.

3. Condition the apples before storing.

To Store

Wrap the dried apples in a paper towel before sealing in a Mylar bag, to prevent them from piercing the bag in storage. Dried apples stored in vacuum-sealed glass jars, or Mylar bags with oxygen absorbers, will keep for up to 5 years.

MIX IT UP: Apples are a versatile fruit. Thinly slice them for snacking chips or pie filling. Slice them a little thicker or dice them to add to trail mix or granola. Toss dried apple cubes into a curry just before serving. The apples will rehydrate in the sauce and add sweetness to the dish.

Apricots

Prep time: 15 minutes / **Dehydration time:** 19 to 24 hours
Yield: 2 pounds fresh = 2 cups dried = 3 cups rehydrated

Dried apricots make great snacks, and rehydrated apricots can be used for both sweet and savory dishes. Choose soft, ripe apricots that are juicy with orange skin.

To Prepare

1. Wash the apricots in cold water with a squirt of dish soap and vinegar. Soak them briefly to remove grime and pesticide residues, then rinse and dry.

2. Cut the apricots in half and remove the pits.

3. Turn each apricot half inside out to expose the center flesh.

4. Soak the halves in ascorbic acid solution or lemon juice for 1 minute, then drain them.

5. Arrange the apricot halves in a single layer, flesh-side up, on the dehydrator trays.

To Dehydrate

1. Dehydrate at 135°F for 4 hours. Reduce the temperature to 125°F and continue drying for 15 to 20 hours.

2. When dried, the apricots should be leathery and pliable, with no spongy centers.

3. Condition the apricots before storing.

To Store

Dried apricots stored in vacuum-sealed glass jars, or Mylar bags with oxygen absorbers, will keep for up to 5 years. Their shelf life is 1 year without oxygen absorbers.

Bananas

Prep time: 10 minutes / **Dehydration time:** 10 to 12 hours
Yield: 10 medium bananas = 2 cups dried = 4 cups rehydrated

Choose firm, ripe bananas that are all yellow or only lightly flecked with brown. Bananas have a strong scent and should be dried on their own in the dehydrator, because their fragrance will permeate any other fruit that shares the dehydrator with them.

To Prepare

1. Cut off both ends of each banana. Remove the peels.

2. Cut away any bruised spots. Slice the bananas into ¼-inch slices for chunks, or ⅛-inch slices for chips.

3. Soak the bananas in citric acid solution or lemon juice for 1 minute, then drain them.

4. Arrange the bananas in a single layer on the dehydrator trays.

To Dehydrate

1. Dehydrate at 135°F for 4 hours. Reduce the temperature to 125°F and continue drying for 6 to 8 hours.

2. When dried, the bananas should be leathery and dry in the center.

3. Condition the bananas before storing.

To Store

Bananas are strongly scented after drying, so they are best stored in glass jars with an oxygen absorber to prevent their scent from transferring to other foods. Bananas stored vacuum-sealed or with oxygen absorbers will keep for 2 to 3 years.

MIX IT UP: Dried bananas taste intensely sweet. Add them to your favorite banana bread or banana muffin recipe and reduce the sugar by half. The dried banana pieces will rehydrate as they bake but remain slightly chewy, lending their sweetness to the baked goods.

Blueberries

Prep time: 10 minutes / **Dehydration time:** 12 to 14 hours
Yield: 2 cups fresh blueberries = ¾ cup dried = 1½ cups rehydrated

Drying blueberries is a terrific way to store a bit of summer's delicious bounty. Choose firm, ripe blueberries to dry and use them in pancakes, muffins, trail mix, bagels, and tea/dessert breads.

To Prepare

1. Wash the blueberries in cold water. Remove any stems and green or misshapen berries.

2. Blanch the blueberries: Place them in a stainless-steel bowl and pour 4 cups of boiling water over them to crack the skins. After 2 minutes, drain the hot water (do not cook the blueberries).

3. Arrange the blueberries in a single layer on a dehydrator tray.

4. The blueberries will drip as they dry, so place a fruit leather sheet on an empty tray below them to catch the drips.

To Dehydrate

1. Dehydrate at 140°F degrees for 4 hours. Reduce the temperature to 130°F and continue drying for 8 to 10 hours.

2. When dried, the blueberries should be firm, leathery, and chewy, with no sponginess in the center.

3. Condition the berries before storing.

To Store

Store dried blueberries in vacuum-sealed glass jars or in Mylar bags with oxygen absorbers. Protect the berries from light and heat in storage. They will keep for up to 5 years.

ELEVATE YOUR DISH: Dried blueberries are sweet on their own, but you can make them even more delicious by adding honey to the blanching water. Use a ratio of 1 cup of honey to 1½ cups of boiled water. Stir to fully dissolve the honey. Use this honey water in place of the boiling water in the recipe.

Cherries

Prep time: 20 minutes / **Dehydration time:** 18 to 22 hours
Yield: 1 pound fresh cherries = 1½ cups dried = 2 cups rehydrated

Choose firm, fully ripe cherries with no insect damage. Dried cherries are naturally sweet like candy, and can be eaten plain or added to trail mix, granola bars, and baked goods.

To Prepare

1. Wash the cherries in cold water and drain them. Remove the stems.

2. Cut the cherries in half and remove the pits (a cherry pitter can speed up this task).

3. Dip pale cherries, like Queen Anne or Rainier, in ascorbic acid solution or lemon juice to prevent them from browning.

4. Arrange the cherry halves in a single layer, flesh-side up, on the dehydrator trays.

To Dehydrate

1. Dehydrate at 145°F for 4 hours. Reduce the temperature to 135°F and continue drying for 14 to 18 hours.

2. Test for doneness when the cherries are cool. When dried, the cherries should be sticky, flexible, and leathery with no sponginess in the flesh when squeezed.

3. Condition the cherries before storing.

To Store

Store dried cherries in vacuum-sealed glass jars, or in Mylar bags with oxygen absorbers. Protect the cherries from light and heat in storage. They will keep for up to 5 years.

ELEVATE YOUR DISH: Rehydrate cherries using brandy or cherry liqueur. Use 1 cup dried fruit to ½ cup liqueur. Allow the dried fruit to rehydrate for 60 minutes. Spoon the alcohol-soaked cherries over ice cream or cheesecake for a delicious dessert topping.

Citus

Prep time: 15 minutes / **Dehydration time:** 6 to 8 hours

Yield: 6 lemons, 10 limes, or 3 medium oranges = 2 cups dried

Organic lemons, limes, and oranges dry quickly—and together!—in the dehydrator. Sliced thin, unpeeled, they make flavorful additions to herbal teas and syrups. Choose thin-skinned citrus varieties like Valencia oranges, tangerines, or Meyer lemons for the best flavor.

To Prepare

1. Wash the citrus in warm water with a squirt of dish soap and vinegar. Soak them briefly to remove grime and pesticide residues, then rinse and dry.

2. Cut off the top and bottom ends of the fruit and discard.

3. Cut the fruit into ⅛-inch (or thinner) slices using a mandoline or sharp knife.

4. Arrange the slices in a single layer on the dehydrator trays.

To Dehydrate

1. Dehydrate at 130°F for 6 to 8 hours.

2. When dried, the citrus slices should be dry and crisp with no juiciness in the flesh of the fruit when it is pinched between your thumb and forefinger. Condition the citrus before storing.

To Store

Store dried slices in glass jars with oxygen absorbers. Citrus slices have a 1- to 2-year shelf life when vacuum-sealed. Without vacuum-sealing, expect the fragrance and flavor in citrus peels to last about 6 months.

Dried citrus may be powdered to use as a flavor enhancer. However, because powder oxidizes quickly, only powder what you will use within a month. To powder, place the citrus slices in a blender and process on high speed for 30 seconds.

MIX IT UP: Dehydrated candied citrus peels are a must for holiday baking. Make your own by simmering citrus peels in a 2:1 ratio of sugar and water for 2 hours. Drain. Then dehydrate the candied peels in a single layer in your dehydrator at 120°F for 4 hours.

Coconut

Prep time: 35 minutes / **Dehydration time:** 12 to 16 hours
Yield: 1 small coconut = 1 cup dehydrated

Dried coconut can be used in baking or cooking. Use it to make coconut milk, too. Choose fresh coconuts that are heavy and still contain liquid. Shake the coconut, and you will hear liquid sloshing around. The fruit should not smell musty or moldy, as this is an indication that the fruit is past its prime.

To Prepare

1. Wash the coconut in cold water. Pat it dry.

2. Pierce one end of the coconut, drain the coconut water into a bowl and set it aside for another use.

3. Using a hammer, hit the fruit firmly to crack the shell around the middle.

4. Steam the broken coconut: Place it in a covered steam basket over a saucepan half filled with water (but not touching the bottom of the steam basket), over medium heat. Steam the coconut for 1 minute to loosen the flesh from the shell.

5. Peel away the brown coconut skin. Coarsely grate the white coconut meat.

6. Line the dehydrator trays with fruit leather inserts. Spread the grated coconut evenly over the prepared trays.

To Dehydrate

1. Dehydrate at 120°F for 12 to 16 hours.

2. When dried, the coconut pieces should be crisp.

To Store

Unsweetened, dehydrated coconut will keep in an airtight container for up to 6 months or in a vacuum-sealed container with an oxygen absorber for 1 year.

MIX IT UP: To sweeten the coconut before drying, in a bowl, pour in 2 tablespoons powdered sugar, 1 tablespoon coconut oil, and 2 tablespoons water per cup of grated coconut. Stir well to combine. Let the coconut absorb the sugar for 15 minutes. Dehydrate according to the recipe.

Cranberries

Prep time: 20 minutes / **Dehydration time:** 10 to 12 hours
Yield: 1 cup fresh cranberries = ¼ cup dried

Cranberries aren't just for holiday dinners. Their tangy flavor is a tasty addition to cookies, muffins, scones, and cheese dips. Savor the tartness of dried cranberries for their antimicrobial and anti-inflammatory health benefits. Lightly sweeten them to increase the appeal. For the most intense flavor, choose ripe, firm berries that are mostly red.

To Prepare

1. Wash the cranberries in cold water and drain until they are no longer dripping.

2. Cut each berry in half.

3. If you want to sweeten the cranberries before dehydrating, place 1 cup of prepared cranberries in a bowl. Cover them with 2 tablespoons honey and 2 tablespoons hot water. Stir the cranberries to coat them. Remove them from the syrup with a slotted spoon.

4. Arrange the cranberries in a single layer on the dehydrator trays.

To Dehydrate

1. Dehydrate at 135°F for 4 hours. Reduce the temperature to 120°F and continue drying for 6 to 8 hours.

2. When dried, the cranberries should be leathery but still pliable, with no spongy areas remaining in the center of the berries.

To Store

Cranberries can be stored in vacuum-sealed glass jars or in Mylar bags with oxygen absorbers. The high acid content of cranberries extends their shelf life up to 5 years in storage.

ELEVATE YOUR DISH: Unsweetened dried cranberries can be reconstituted in apple juice or orange juice to add a little sweetness without taking away from their health benefits.

Dates

Prep time: 15 minutes / **Dehydration time:** 8 to 12 hours
Yield: 1 cup fresh dates = 1 cup dried

Fresh dates are rich in natural sugars, and dehydrating them intensifies their sweetness. For dehydrating, choose dark red or brown dates that are plump and firm.

To Prepare

1. Wash the dates under cold running water to remove any dirt and grime. Pat them dry.

2. Cut the dates lengthwise through the center, just to the pit. Remove the pits, but leave the dates whole if you plan on stuffing them later. Or cut the dates in half to speed up the drying time.

3. Arrange the dates in a single layer, cut-side up (if halving), on the dehydrator trays.

To Dehydrate

1. Dehydrate at 145°F for 8 to 12 hours or until they reach the desired doneness. Turn the dates over after 6 hours to ensure even drying. As an optional step, increase the dehydrator to 165°F for the last hour of drying to create a glossy finish on whole dates.

2. When dried, dates should be leathery and chewy.

To Store

Dried dates last for up to 5 years or more when stored in vacuum-sealed glass jars or in Mylar bags with oxygen absorbers. Dates may get a sugary white coating in storage. This sugar will reabsorb if the dates are warmed briefly.

ELEVATE YOUR DISH: Take advantage of the high sugar content of dates by making date sugar. Cut fresh dates into ¼-inch cubes. Dehydrate at 145°F for 20 hours, or until the dates are hard. Cool the dates to room temperature. In a high-powered blender, process the dates to a fine powder. Use this date sugar as a substitute for brown sugar. Its storage and shelf life are the same as dried dates.

Figs

Prep time: 15 minutes / **Dehydration time:** 24 hours
Yield: 9 medium figs = 1 cup dried

Figs are easy to dry with little preparation. Select firm, fully ripe figs for drying. Use them in any recipe that calls for dates or prunes.

To Prepare

1. Wash the figs in cold water and drain them. Remove the stems and cut out any blemishes or bruised parts.

2. Smaller figs can be dried whole; prick the skin with a toothpick in several places. Cut larger figs into halves or quarters.

3. Arrange the figs in a single layer, skin-side down (if halving or quartering), on the dehydrator trays.

To Dehydrate

1. Dehydrate at 135°F for 4 hours. Reduce the temperature to 125°F and continue drying for 20 hours.

2. When dried, the figs should be leathery, flexible, and sticky with no spongy or damp spots.

To Store

Due to their high sugar content, dried figs store well. Store them in vacuum-sealed glass jars or in Mylar bags with oxygen absorbers. Protect the figs from light and heat in storage. They will keep for up to 5 years.

Grapes

Prep time: 15 minutes / **Dehydration time:** 19 to 24 hours
Yield: 1 cup grapes = ¼ cup raisins

Dried grapes are . . . raisins! When dried at home, they taste just like fresh grapes, without the sulfur flavor of store-bought, packaged raisins. Raisins do not rehydrate into grapes, though. Choose organically grown, seedless grapes that are firm and unblemished.

To Prepare

1. Wash the grapes in cold water with a squirt of dish soap and vinegar. Soak them briefly to remove grime and pesticide residues, then rinse and dry.

2. Remove the stems from the grapes. Cut the grapes in half. If your grapes contain seeds, remove them.

3. Arrange the grape halves in a single layer, skin-side down, on the dehydrator trays.

To Dehydrate

1. Dehydrate at 135°F for 4 hours. Reduce the temperature to 125°F and continue drying for 15 to 20 hours, or until the raisins are dry and no soft, spongy areas remain.

2. When dried, the raisins will be shriveled, leathery, and flexible.

3. Cool to room temperature and condition the raisins to even out the moisture level.

To Store

Store raisins in vacuum-sealed glass jars or in Mylar bags with an oxygen absorber. Raisins will keep for 4 to 5 years if stored in a cool, dry place, protected from light and heat. In storage, raisins sometimes have sugar crystals form on the surface. This is safe and doesn't affect the flavor of the raisins. Merely rehydrate the raisins overnight by enclosing them in a plastic bag with a just-damp paper towel to remove the sugar crystals.

Kiwi

Prep time: 15 minutes / **Dehydration time:** 10 to 12 hours
Yield: 5 medium kiwis = 1 cup dried = 1½ cups rehydrated

Kiwi is a tropical fruit with a complex, sweet-tart flavor; when dried, the flavor intensifies. Kiwi will continue to ripen off the vine, so if your kiwi is too hard when you bring it home, place it in a brown paper bag to encourage ripening. You can then process for drying when the kiwis are soft but still somewhat firm.

To Prepare

1. Wash the kiwi in warm water. Pat them dry.

2. If you dislike the fuzzy peel, remove it (the peel can also be left on).

3. Cut the kiwi into ⅛- to ¼-inch slices. (Thinner slices will dry more quickly.)

4. Dip the slices in ascorbic acid solution or lemon juice to prevent browning.

5. Arrange the slices in a single layer on the dehydrator trays. The kiwi slices should not touch each other.

To Dehydrate

1. Dehydrate at 135°F for 4 hours. Reduce the temperature to 125°F and continue drying for 6 to 8 hours.

2. When dried, the kiwi should be leathery and chewy with no spongy areas.

3. Cool the kiwi slices to room temperature. Condition them to even out the moisture levels.

To Store

Store dried kiwi in vacuum-sealed glass jars or in Mylar bags with oxygen absorbers. Store them in a cool, dry place, protected from light and heat. Dried kiwi slices will remain tasty and brightly colored for up to 5 years.

Mangos & Papayas

Prep time: 10 minutes / **Dehydration time:** 14 to 16 hours
Yield: 2 fresh mangos or papayas = 1 cup dried = 1½ cups rehydrated

When they are ripe, mangos and papayas have a sweet, fruity fragrance near the stem. The color of the mango should be bright, although the color may be green, red, or yellow, depending on the variety. Papayas will be 80 percent yellow at their peak of ripeness. Mangos and papayas continue to ripen after picking. To encourage this, place the fruit inside a paper bag with an apple or a banana.

To Prepare

1. Wash mangos or papayas under cool water. Pat them dry.

2. Peel and remove the seed(s).

3. Slice the fruit into ¼-inch to ⅜-inch slices.

4. Place fruit leather sheets on the dehydrator trays to prevent sticking. Arrange the slices in a single layer on the dehydrator trays.

To Dehydrate

1. Dehydrate at 140°F for 4 hours. Reduce the temperature to 130°F and continue drying for 10 to 12 hours.

2. When dried, mangos and papayas should be leathery and pliable with no spongy, moist areas; the fruit will not be sticky.

To Store

Store dried mangos in vacuum-sealed glass jars or in Mylar bags with oxygen absorbers. Protect from light to preserve the color of the dried fruit, which keeps for up to 5 years.

MIX IT UP: Use papaya seeds to make a pepper-like spice. Rinse the seeds in a colander to remove the slimy coating and any residual fruit pulp. Spread the seeds on a fruit leather sheet on a dehydrator tray. Dehydrate at 105°F for 4 to 6 hours or until the seeds are dry and brittle. Powder the papaya seeds in a blender on high speed for 30 seconds. Papaya seeds are high in antioxidants and promote digestive health.

Melons

Prep time: 15 minutes / **Dehydration time:** 12 to 15 hours
Yield: 1 medium melon = 2 cups dehydrated = 3 cups rehydrated

There are more than 40 different kinds of melons, even though grocery stores only carry a few. Melons are predominantly water, so they shrink dramatically during drying. Dehydrating concentrates the sugars in the fruit, intensifying the sweet flavors. Choose vine-ripened, sweet melons with firm flesh. Ripe melons will have a sweet, fruity fragrance at the stem end and a pale, cream-colored area on one side, where they rested on the ground as they grew.

To Prepare

1. Wash the melon under warm, soapy water. Use a brush to remove any dirt on the surface. Rinse well. Pat it dry.

2. Cut the melon in half and remove the seeds.

3. Peel the melon and slice it into ½-inch slices or cubes.

4. Arrange the melon slices in a single layer on the dehydrator trays.

To Dehydrate

1. Dehydrate at 125°F for 12 to 15 hours. Flip the fruit after 6 hours, to ensure even drying.

2. When dried, cantaloupe and honeydew melon should be leathery and pliable with no stickiness. (The fruit will lose a lot of volume during the drying process.)

To Store

Melons have a shorter storage life than other dried fruit. When stored in vacuum-sealed glass jars or in Mylar bags with oxygen absorbers, they should last for up to 2 years. To preserve their color, protect dried melons from the light.

Peaches & Nectarines

Prep time: 20 minutes / **Dehydration time:** 14 to 16 hours
Yield: 3 peaches or nectarines = 1½ cups dried = 2 cups rehydrated

Choose ripe peaches or nectarines that are firm but give to gentle pressure. Choose freestone and semi-freestone varieties, such as Elegant Lady or Red Haven, to save effort in removing the pit from the peach. Freestone peaches release their pit from the flesh of the peach easily, whereas clingstone peach varieties, such as Early Sunrise, cling to the pit and must be cut away with a knife.

To Prepare

1. Wash the peaches or nectarines in cold water to remove any grime.

2. Blanch the peaches to remove the fuzzy skin: Submerge them in boiling water for 1 minute, then plunge them in cold water to prevent the fruit from cooking. The skins will slip off easily. Nectarines can be dried with the skin on.

3. Cut the fruit in half and remove the pit. Slice the fruit into uniform, ¼-inch slices.

4. Soak the slices in ascorbic acid solution for 3 minutes, then drain them.

5. Arrange the slices in a single layer on the dehydrator sheets.

To Dehydrate

1. Dehydrate at 135°F for 4 hours. Reduce the temperature to 120°F and continue drying for 10 to 12 hours.

2. Halfway through the drying time, rotate the trays and turn the slices over to expose the bottom side.

3. Peaches and nectarines darken easily during processing. If your fruit begins to darken and caramelize, reduce the temperature to 110°F and continue drying.

4. When dried, the peaches and nectarines should be leathery and chewy.

5. Condition the fruit before packaging.

To Store

Dried peaches and nectarines stored in vacuum-sealed glass jars, or in Mylar bags with oxygen absorbers, will keep for up to 5 years. The hard edges of the fruit may puncture Mylar bags; to prevent this, insert a paper towel between the fruit and the sides of the bag.

Pears

Prep time: 10 minutes / **Dehydration time:** 16 to 24 hours
Yield: 1 pound pears = 1 cup dried = 1½ cups rehydrated

Chewy and sweet, pears are easy to dehydrate. Summer and early-fall pear varieties like Bartlett or Lincoln are best for dehydrating. Winter pears, such as D'Anjou or Bosc, have a grainier texture but may also be dried. Choose pale green pears and allow them to ripen on the kitchen counter over a few days, until they gradually turn yellow. Pears are at their best when they are barely yellow and still firm, and the stem easily pulls from the fruit.

To Prepare

1. Wash the pears in cold water. Pat them dry.

2. There is no need to peel the pears. Slice them in quarters and remove the stem and core with a knife. Cut each quarter into ¼-inch slices.

3. To prevent browning, dip the pieces in an ascorbic acid solution or lemon juice for 5 seconds. Drain.

4. Arrange the pieces in a single layer on the dehydrator trays.

To Dehydrate

1. Dehydrate at 135°F for 4 hours. Reduce the temperature to 125°F and continue drying for 12 to 20 hours. Pears with a higher juice content, like Bartletts, will take longer to dehydrate.

2. When dried, the pears should be leathery and pliable with no moist or spongy areas remaining.

To Store

Dried pears stored in vacuum-sealed glass jars, or in Mylar bags with oxygen absorbers, will keep for up to 5 years. The hard edges of the fruit may puncture Mylar bags; to prevent this, insert a paper towel between the fruit and the sides of the bag.

MIX IT UP: Dip dehydrated pears in dark chocolate and harden on parchment paper for a simple but elegant snack.

Peas & Chickpeas

Prep time: 25 minutes / **Dehydration time:** 6 to 8 hours
Yield: 1 pound fresh green peas in the pod = ⅓ cup dried = 1 cup rehydrated

Peas and chickpeas are pantry staples. Whether you grow your own or buy from the farmers' market, you'll be starting with peas in a pod (see the Mix It Up tip for how to dehydrate frozen peas). For the sweetest peas, look for firm but juicy green pods that are just barely filled out and still flexible. Tender peas should be processed quickly after picking. They become starchy and mealy within a few hours of harvest. Fresh chickpeas are treated in the same way as fresh green peas.

To Prepare

1. Wash the pea pods in a sink of cold water. Drain.

2. Shell the peas from the pod, reserving the tender peas and discarding the pods.

3. Blanch the peas: Boil them for 4 minutes or until the color of the peas brightens. Remove the peas from the boiling water and submerge them immediately in cold water to cool. Drain the peas.

4. Arrange the peas in a single layer on the dehydrator trays.

To Dehydrate

1. Dehydrate at 125°F for 6 to 8 hours.

2. When dried, the peas should be hard and brittle.

To Store

Dried peas stored in glass jars or in Mylar bags with oxygen absorbers will keep for 4 to 5 years.

MIX IT UP: Dehydrate frozen peas for a shelf-stable addition to your pantry. Frozen peas have already been shelled and blanched, so when you start with frozen peas, you save time. Arrange the frozen peas in a single layer on the dehydrator trays. Dehydrate at 125°F for 6 to 8 hours.

Pineapples

Prep time: 20 minutes / **Dehydration time:** 14 to 18 hours
Yield: 1 medium fresh pineapple = 2½ cups dehydrated = 3½ cups rehydrated

Pineapples are a sweet addition to trail mix, granola, muffins, and breads. When choosing a ripe pineapple, look for fresh, glossy leaves. The skin should be yellowish brown and the fruit should be free of mold or gray areas around the stem end. A fully ripe pineapple will smell fruity and sweet near the base; if the pineapple is scentless or smells "off," look for a better candidate.

To Prepare

1. Wash the pineapple with cold water. Pat it dry.

2. Cut off the leafy top and the bottom of the pineapple. Cut it into quarters. With a sharp knife, cut away the core and the hard skin.

3. Cut the pineapple meat into ½-inch wedges or ¼-inch slices. Keep the cuts uniform for even dehydrating.

4. Arrange the pineapple in a single layer on the dehydrator trays.

To Dehydrate

1. Dehydrate at 140°F for 4 hours. Reduce the temperature to 130°F and continue drying for 10 to 14 hours. Rotate the dehydrator trays after 8 hours to ensure even drying.

2. When dried, the pineapple should be leathery and pliable, with no sticky or spongy areas.

To Store

Store dried pineapple in vacuum-sealed glass jars or in Mylar bags with oxygen absorbers. When stored below 70°F and protected from light and heat, the pineapple will keep for 5 years or more.

Plums & Prune Plums

Prep time: 15 minutes / **Dehydration time:** 24 hours
Yield: 1 pound plums = 1½ cups dried = 2 cups rehydrated

All dried plums are prunes, but smaller Italian plums are the choicest plums for making prunes due to their smaller size. Choose firm plums that yield slightly under pressure. Rock-hard plums were picked too soon and will lack flavor. Ripe prune plums have dark purple skin with deep-amber-colored flesh.

To Prepare

1. Wash the fruit in cold water. Pat it dry.

2. Cut the fruit in half and remove the pits. Turn each half inside out, with the flesh side pushed out.

3. Arrange the halves in a single layer, flesh-side up, on the dehydrator trays.

To Dehydrate

1. Dehydrate at 135°F for 4 hours. Reduce the temperature to 125°F and continue drying for 20 hours.

2. When dried, the prunes should be leathery and flexible, with no moist or sticky areas. They will be drier and more leathery than commercial dried prunes.

To Store

Prunes stored in vacuum-sealed glass jars, or Mylar bags with oxygen absorbers, will keep for up to 5 years. To preserve their color, store them in a cool, dry place protected from light.

ELEVATE YOUR DISH: Stewed prunes are plump and syrupy. To make them, add 1 cup of dried prunes, 2 teaspoons of lemon juice, and 1½ cups of water to a saucepan. Bring to a boil and turn down the heat. Simmer on low for 20 minutes until the plums are plump and syrupy. Add honey to taste. Serve warm.

Pumpkin & Sunflower Seeds

Prep time: 5 minutes, plus 6 hours to soak / **Dehydration time:** 12 to 15 hours
Yield: 1 cup raw seeds, shelled = 1 cup dehydrated

To make raw pumpkin seeds and sunflower seeds more digestible, they need to be soaked to remove enzyme inhibitors. Choose shelled, raw sunflower seeds and raw pumpkin seeds for drying. Eat the dehydrated seeds as a snack or use them in any recipe that calls for tasty crunch.

To Prepare

1. Rinse the seeds and remove any pieces of shell or broken seeds.

2. Place the seeds in a bowl and cover with cold water. Cover the bowl with a lid or with plastic wrap.

3. Soak the seeds for 6 hours. Then rinse them under cold, running water until there is no more foaming, which indicates that the enzyme inhibitors have been removed.

4. Line a dehydrator tray with a fruit leather sheet.

5. Arrange the seeds in a single layer on the dehydrator tray.

To Dehydrate

1. To maintain the nutritional quality of the seeds, dehydrate at 115°F for 12 to 15 hours. The lower temperatures dry the seeds more slowly but preserve the nutrients in the seeds.

2. When dried, the seeds should be crisp.

To Store

Store the dried sunflower seeds and pumpkin seeds in an airtight container at room temperature, and plan to use them within 3 months. Or freeze them in an airtight container to extend the shelf life up to a year.

ELEVATE YOUR DISH: To the soaking water, add 1 tablespoon of Himalayan salt per 4 cups of seeds. After rinsing—but before dehydrating—sprinkle the seeds with herbs and spices for a more delicious snack. Try ginger-lemon powder, Chipotle Peppers & Smoked Paprika (page 85) and lime juice, or your favorite dry salad dressing mix.

Raspberries & Blackberries

Prep time: 5 minutes / **Dehydration time:** 16 to 19 hours
Yield: 1 pint basket of berries = 1 cup dried = 1¼ cups rehydrated

Raspberries and blackberries intensify in flavor after dehydrating. Because they have a lot of juice, they become light and airy after dehydrating. Choose perfectly ripe, unblemished berries with strong color for dehydrating. These do not continue to ripen after picking.

To Prepare

1. If possible, do not wash the berries before dehydrating them. If you purchased the fruit at a grocery store, wash the fruit briefly under running water. Remove any unripe green berries.

2. Arrange the berries in a single layer, stem-end down, on the dehydrator trays and drain until they are no longer dripping before turning on the dehydrator.

To Dehydrate

1. Dehydrate at 135°F for 4 hours. Reduce the temperature to 125°F and continue drying for 12 to 15 hours.

2. When dried, the berries should be airy and brittle. They will powder easily.

To Store

Dehydrated berries are best stored in vacuum-sealed glass jars. They are fragile and will not remain intact in Mylar bags. If protected from light and heat, they will keep for up to 2 years.

MIX IT UP: Dehydrated berries are intensely flavorful and powder easily. They are rich in antioxidants with a low-glycemic level, making them an ideal addition to morning smoothies. Put the dried berries in a blender and pulse to make berry powder. Use 1 tablespoon of powder per serving of smoothie.

Rhubarb

Prep time: 20 minutes / **Dehydration time:** 10 hours
Yield: 1 pound rhubarb = 1 cup dried = 1½ cups rehydrated

Rhubarb is an old garden vegetable that is treated like a fruit. The stems are tart and astringent with a unique, thirst-quenching quality (but do not eat the leaves, as these can be toxic). Different varieties of rhubarb have different-colored stems, so the color is not an indication of ripeness. Choose firm, juicy stems that are heavy for their size.

To Prepare

1. Cut off the leaf and the root end of each stalk and discard those parts. Wash the rhubarb stems in cold water to remove the soil. Pat them dry.

2. Cut each stem into ½-inch pieces.

3. Blanch the rhubarb: In a saucepan, combine 1 cup sugar, 1 cup honey, and 2 cups water, and bring to a boil. (Or use a simple syrup, see the Elevate Your Dish tip on page 89.) Add the rhubarb pieces and boil for 1 minute. Drain the blanched rhubarb.

4. Arrange the pieces in a single layer on the dehydrator trays.

To Dehydrate

1. Dehydrate at 135°F for 4 hours. Reduce the temperature to 125°F and continue drying for 6 hours.

2. When dried, the rhubarb should be leathery and stiff.

To Store

Rhubarb stored in vacuum-sealed glass jars, or Mylar bags with oxygen absorbers, will keep for up to 5 years. To preserve its color, store in a cool, dry place, protected from light.

Strawberries

Prep time: 15 minutes / **Dehydration time:** 12 to 16 hours
Yield: 1 pound strawberries = 1 cup dried = 1 cup rehydrated

Choose ripe strawberries that are red, juicy, with deep-red flesh for the best flavor after drying. Dehydrating intensifies the flavor of strawberries and gives them a pleasant, chewy texture.

To Prepare

1. Wash the strawberries in cold water with a squirt of dish soap and vinegar. Soak them briefly to remove dirt and pesticide residues, then rinse and dry.

2. Remove the green tops using a sharp knife (see the Mix It Up tip).

3. Slice the strawberries into ¼-inch slices.

4. Arrange the strawberry slices in a single layer on the dehydrator trays.

To Dehydrate

1. Dehydrate at 135°F for 4 hours. Reduce the temperature to 125°F and continue drying for 8 to 12 hours.

2. When dried, the strawberries should be leathery but pliable, with no moist or spongy areas.

To Store

Store dried strawberries in vacuum-sealed glass jars or in Mylar bags with oxygen absorbers. When they are stored away from light and heat, their shelf life is up to 5 years.

MIX IT UP: As you are preparing your strawberries for drying, don't discard the tops. They can be dried for tea. Leaving a little extra fruit attached enhances the flavor. Slice the tops cleanly from the fruit, and dry at 105°F for 6 hours or overnight. The flavor is especially good with lemon balm, lemongrass, or hibiscus in an herbal tea blend.

Tree Nuts & Peanuts

Prep time: 15 minutes, plus 12 hours to soak / **Dehydration time:** 16 to 19 hours
Yield: 1 cup raw nuts = 1 cup dehydrated nuts

Walnuts, pecans, almonds, and peanuts are delicious and nutritious snacks. But they contain antinutrients that can cause digestive trouble. Soaking them, and then dehydrating them, removes these enzyme inhibitors, making them easier to digest. Choose well-formed, raw tree nuts and peanuts.

To Prepare

1. Shell and sort the nuts, discarding any that are discolored, misshapen, or imperfect.

2. Soak the nuts in enough salted water to cover them by 2 inches. Use 1 tablespoon of salt to 4 cups nuts. Soak for 12 hours. Drain and rinse the nuts to remove any salt residue.

3. Arrange the nuts in a single layer on the dehydrator trays.

To Dehydrate

1. Dehydrate at 115°F for 4 hours. Reduce the temperature to 105°F and continue drying for 12 to 15 hours.

2. When dried, the nuts should be crisp.

To Store

Dehydrated raw nuts have a short shelf life due to the oils in the nuts. Store them in an airtight container for up to 3 months in the refrigerator, or freeze them for up to a year.

MIX IT UP: Nuts can be roasted after dehydrating or used to make nut butters. To roast the nuts, place them in a single layer on a dry baking sheet. Roast them at 375°F for 10 minutes or until they are fragrant and lightly brown. Make nut butter by placing 2 cups cooled, roasted nuts and ¼ cup oil in a blender or food processor. Pulse the machine at 10-second intervals, scraping as needed, until the nut butter is the consistency you desire.

Watermelon

Prep time: 15 minutes / **Dehydration time:** 12 to 15 hours
Yield: 4 wedges from a medium watermelon = ½ cup dehydrated = 1 cup rehydrated

Watermelons, like other melons, are predominantly water. They shrink dramatically during drying. Dehydrating concentrates the sugars in fruit, intensifying the sweet flavors. Ripe watermelons sound hollow when thumped gently and have a pale, cream-colored area on one side, where they rested on the ground as they grew.

To Prepare

1. Wash the watermelon under warm, soapy water. Rinse well and pat it dry.

2. Cut the melon into ½-inch-thick slices and remove the seeds.

3. Cut the rind away from the flesh and discard. Slice the watermelon into ½-inch slices or cubes.

4. Arrange the watermelon in a single layer on the dehydrator trays.

To Dehydrate

1. Dehydrate at 135°F for 12 to 15 hours.

2. Flip the melon pieces after 6 hours to ensure even drying.

3. When dried, the watermelon should be sticky and pliable, much like fruit leather.

To Store

Watermelons, with their high sugar content, have a shorter storage life than other fruit. When packaged in vacuum-sealed glass jars, or Mylar bags with oxygen absorbers, they should last for up to 2 years. To preserve their color, protect dried watermelon from light.

CHAPTER 4

Dehydrating Vegetables

Vegetables are rich in vitamins and antioxidants that reduce the risk of diseases, including cancer. Drying vegetables at their peak of freshness preserves these nutrients for future meals. Dried vegetables can be used in a variety of ways, such as side dishes, snacks, or ingredients in soups and stews. Powdered, dried vegetables add a punch of flavor and nutrition to shakes, smoothies, and even desserts.

All vegetables to be dried should be free of blemishes, soft spots, and mold. Vegetables that are past their prime will not improve in the dehydrator and may introduce off-flavors when cooked.

Wash vegetables in cold water to prepare them for dehydrating. Avoid prolonged soaking, as this can leach water-soluble vitamins from the vegetables and speed up deterioration. Use a vegetable brush to gently remove dirt from young root vegetables, rather than peeling, as many nutrients are located just under the skin.

Blanching vegetables helps them retain their color, texture, and flavor during the drying process and shortens drying times. However, not all vegetables require blanching. Refer to the individual recipes for precise directions.

Cutting vegetables into uniform pieces will help ensure even drying (use a food processor or mandoline to help with this). When all the pieces are small and uniform, the drying time is shorter and the vegetables are more flavorful and tender. Because vegetables contain less moisture than fruit, dry them at lower temperatures to prevent "case hardening." When case hardening occurs, the outside of the vegetable dries and prevents the moisture on the inside from escaping. Case-hardened vegetables appear dry but feel spongy in the center. Generally, vegetables are dried at 125°F.

Vegetables shrink and curl as they dry. You may find vegetables falling through the holes on some dehydrator trays as they dry. If your dehydrator has larger holes, use a tray liner to help keep veggies from falling through.

Vegetables will be leathery and brittle when they are completely dry. They will snap cleanly when bent, or crumble when crushed. Refer to individual recipes for exact instructions.

Beans (Green, Wax & Snap)

Prep time: 15 minutes / **Dehydration time:** 10 to 12 hours
Yield: 1 pound of beans = 1½ cups dehydrated = 3 cups rehydrated

Since the eighteenth century, dried green beans have been called "leather britches" because they split open along the seam when they dry, resembling a pair of pants. Green, purple, red, and yellow beans are all suitable for dehydrating. After blanching, both purple and red beans will turn green. For the best texture and flavor, choose full-size, plump beans with little seed development.

To Prepare

1. Wash the beans in cold water. Trim the tips and tail ends from each bean. Some heritage bean varieties have a fibrous string running down the seam of the bean. Remove that by pulling it from the stem end to the tip of the bean. It will come off easily.

2. Cut the beans into 1½-inch lengths.

3. Blanch the beans in a pot of boiling water for 2 to 3 minutes. Purple and red beans will turn bright green. Green beans will brighten in color. Remove the beans from the blanching water with a slotted spoon. Place the beans in ice water to cool. Drain the beans in a colander.

4. Arrange the beans in a single layer on the dehydrator trays.

To Dehydrate

1. Dehydrate at 135°F for 10 to 12 hours.

2. When dried, the beans should be hard and brittle.

To Store

Dried beans stored in vacuum-sealed glass jars, or Mylar bags with oxygen absorbers, will keep for up to 5 years.

Beets

Prep and cook time: 1 hour / **Dehydration time:** 10 to 12 hours
Yield: 4 medium beets (1 pound) = 1 cup dried = 1½ cups rehydrated

Beets are sweeter in the fall and winter. Choose firm, heavy roots that are well formed, with no side shoots. Baking beets before dehydrating them concentrates the sugars and enhances the flavor.

To Prepare

1. Wash the beets in cold water. Using a vegetable brush, remove any dirt from the roots. Cut off the leafy green tops, leaving ¼ inch close to the root (the beets will bleed if the top is cut off).

2. Preheat the oven to 300°F. Line a baking sheet with parchment paper. Place the whole beets on the prepared baking sheet. Bake for 30 minutes, or until the beets are tender when pricked with a fork. Remove the beets from the oven.

3. Chill the beets in ice water for 5 minutes.

4. With the beets still in the cold water, peel the beets by slipping the skin from the roots with your fingers. If the skins don't slip off easily, use a paring knife to scrape the skins from the roots.

5. Slice the beets into ¼-inch slices or coarsely cube them.

6. Arrange the beets in a single layer on the dehydrator trays. Place a lined tray under the last tray of beets to catch any drips and prevent the beets from discoloring any vegetables below them in the dehydrator.

To Dehydrate

1. Dehydrate at 125°F for 10 to 12 hours.

2. Cool the beets to room temperature to test for doneness. When dried, the beets should be leathery and hard.

To Store

Dried beets stored in vacuum-sealed glass jars, or in Mylar bags with oxygen absorbers, will keep for up to 5 years. The hard edges of the beets may puncture the Mylar bags. Insert a paper towel in the Mylar bag between the beets and the sides of the bag to prevent punctures.

Broccoli & Cauliflower

Prep time: 15 minutes / **Dehydration time:** 12 to 14 hours

Yield: 1 medium head broccoli or cauliflower = 1 cup dried = 1½ cups rehydrated

Broccoli and cauliflower are rich in sulforaphane, an antioxidant that helps the body fight cancer. Choose heads of broccoli or cauliflower with dense buds that are tightly closed. Broccoli should be a deep green color, and cauliflower should be pearly white with no brown spots.

To Prepare

1. Wash the broccoli or cauliflower in cold water. If you are using organic broccoli or cauliflower, soak the heads in a bowl of water with 1 tablespoon of added salt for 5 minutes to remove any bugs. Rinse well to remove the salt.

2. Cut the head to separate the florets from the stalk. Cut the florets into ½-inch-thick pieces. Cut the stalks in half lengthwise, and cut each half into ½-inch slices.

3. Place the florets into a covered steam basket over a pot of boiling water. Steam the broccoli or cauliflower for 2 minutes to blanch it. The broccoli will turn bright green when it is fully blanched. The cauliflower will become slightly translucent when done. Rinse it with cold water to stop the blanching process.

4. Arrange the prepared broccoli or cauliflower in a single layer on the dehydrator trays.

To Dehydrate

1. Dehydrate at 125°F for 12 to 14 hours.

2. When dried, the broccoli and cauliflower should be brittle and crumbly.

To Store

Both dried broccoli and cauliflower stored in vacuum-sealed glass jars, or in Mylar bags with oxygen absorbers, will keep for up to 5 years.

Cabbage & Brussels Sprouts

Prep time: 15 minutes / **Dehydration time:** 8 to 12 hours
Yield: 1 pound cabbage or Brussels sprouts = 1 cup dried = 2 cups rehydrated

Cabbage and Brussels sprouts are best in the fall and winter, after they've had a frost; their color will be more vibrant and their flavor will be sweeter. Choose cabbages with dense, heavy heads and tight leaves. Savoy, red, napa, and green cabbages are the best choices for dehydrating.

To Prepare

1. Remove the coarse outer leaves of both cabbage and Brussels sprouts. Wash under cold running water to remove any dirt.

2. Cut the Brussels sprouts in half lengthwise. Cut the cabbage in quarters lengthwise and remove the core. Using a food processor or grater, shred the cabbage into thin strips.

3. Steam the Brussels sprouts and prepared cabbage in a covered steam basket placed over a pot of boiling water for 2 minutes to blanch. The vegetables will become limp and translucent when done. Chill under cold running water to stop the blanching process. Drain the vegetables.

4. Arrange the Brussels sprout halves in a single layer on the dehydrator trays. Shredded cabbage can be mounded up in a thin layer on the dehydrator trays. It will shrink while drying.

To Dehydrate

1. Dehydrate at 135°F for 8 to 12 hours. Stir the shredded cabbage after 4 hours to encourage even drying.

2. When dried, the dehydrated cabbage and Brussels sprouts will be crisp and brittle. The thicker ribs of the cabbage take longer to dry than the leafy parts.

To Store

Dried cabbage or Brussels sprouts stored in vacuum-sealed glass jars, or in Mylar bags with oxygen absorbers, will keep for up to 2 years.

MIX IT UP: To extend its shelf life, fermented cabbage and sauerkraut can be dehydrated in much the same way as shredded fresh cabbage. To preserve the beneficial bacteria, dehydrate sauerkraut at 105°F for 14 hours or until it is brittle and crumbly.

Carrots & Root Vegetables

Prep time: 15 minutes / **Dehydration time:** 10 to 12 hours
Yield: 4 medium carrots = 1 cup dried = 1½ cups rehydrated

Carrots and other root vegetables are sweetest in the fall and winter. Choose firm, heavy roots that are well formed, with no side shoots.

To Prepare

1. Wash the carrots and other root vegetables in cold water. If the skin of the carrot is dry and thick, peel with a vegetable peeler. Thin-skinned carrots may be scraped with the edge of a paring knife to remove any dirt and a fine layer of peel.

2. Slice the carrots and other root vegetables into ¼-inch slices, or coarsely cube them.

3. Steam the prepared vegetables by placing them in a covered steam basket over a pot of boiling water for 2 minutes until the vegetables are tender-crisp when tested with a fork. Chill them in cold water to stop the cooking process. Drain the vegetables.

4. Arrange the prepared vegetables in a single layer on the dehydrator trays.

To Dehydrate

1. Dehydrate at 125°F for 10 to 12 hours.

2. When dried, the carrots and root vegetables will be leathery and hard.

3. Fully cool before packaging to store.

To Store

Dried root vegetables stored in vacuum-sealed glass jars, or in Mylar bags with oxygen absorbers, will keep for up to 5 years.

ELEVATE YOUR DISH: The sweetness of root vegetables can be enhanced by roasting them before dehydrating. Prepare the root vegetables as above, but skip the blanching step. Instead, arrange them in a single layer on a baking sheet. Bake them in a 400°F oven for 20 minutes, or until they are tender when pricked with a fork. Cool them to room temperature before dehydrating.

Celery

Prep time: 10 minutes / **Dehydration time:** 8 hours
Yield: 6 celery stalks = 1 cup dried = 1½ cups rehydrated

Dried celery is a key ingredient in flavorful soups and sauces in many cuisines. Choose moist, fresh celery that is still juicy on the inside. Older celery stalks that are white and pithy on the inside can be used, but they will not be as aromatic (see the Elevate Your Dish tip).

To Prepare

1. Cut off the bottom of the celery in one piece and discard. Wash the individual celery stalks, paying particular attention to the area at the base of the stalk where dirt accumulates.

2. Cut off the leafy celery tops from the large celery stalks. The thinner stalks with their leaves dry more quickly. Cut the thin stalks with their leaves crosswise into ½-inch pieces, and dry them on separate trays from the main celery stalks so you can dry them more efficiently. Slice the thicker celery stalk crosswise into ¼-inch slices.

3. Arrange the celery in a single layer on the dehydrator trays.

To Dehydrate

1. Dehydrate at 125°F. The leafy tops will take about 4 hours to dry. The thicker stalks will dry in about 8 hours.

2. When dried, the celery should be crisp and brittle.

To Store

Dried celery stored in vacuum-sealed glass jars, or in Mylar bags with oxygen absorbers, will keep for up to 5 years.

ELEVATE YOUR DISH: The Cajun aromatic vegetable blend, the "Cajun Trinity," consists of equal parts celery, sweet bell peppers, and onions. It is an essential ingredient in Cajun and Creole soups, gumbos, and rice dishes. Dry these aromatic vegetables separately and combine them in a jar so you can conveniently add their flavors and aroma to your cooking.

Corn

Prep time: 20 minutes / **Dehydration time:** 8 to 10 hours
Yield: 3 ears of corn or 2 cups corn kernels = 1 cup dehydrated = 1½ cups rehydrated

Sweet corn can be used as a vegetable in soups or salsa, or ground into flour and used in corn tortillas, polenta, or corn chips. Choose heavy, full ears of corn with deep-green leaves.

To Prepare

1. Remove the leaves and silk strands from each ear of corn. Trim the stalk from the bottom of the corn cob. Wash the corn in cold water.

2. Cook whole cobs in a pot of boiling water until tender, about 6 minutes. Cool in cold water.

3. Use a sharp knife to cut the kernels of corn from the cobs.

4. Arrange the kernels in a single layer on the dehydrator trays.

To Dehydrate

1. Dehydrate at 135°F for 8 to 10 hours.

2. When dried, the corn should be hard and brittle.

To Store

Store dried corn in vacuum-sealed glass jars or Mylar bags with oxygen absorbers. When protected from light and heat in storage, it will keep for up to 5 years.

MIX IT UP: Save time by starting with frozen corn. Frozen corn has already been cleaned and blanched. Spread the corn on your dehydrator trays while still frozen. Add 1 hour to the drying time to compensate for the ice in the frozen corn.

Cucumbers

Prep time: 10 minutes / **Dehydration time:** 6 to 8 hours
Yield: 1 cucumber = ½ cup dehydrated = 1 cup rehydrated

Dried cucumbers add their fresh summer flavor to salad dressings, dips, and smoothies. Choose English and Japanese cucumbers with sweet flavors, smooth skins, and immature seeds for the best texture and flavor. Other cucumber varieties may also be dried, provided that the seeds are undeveloped.

To Prepare

1. Wash the cucumbers in cold water. If you are using garden cucumbers, peel the cucumber to remove the bitter skin. Thinner-skinned English or Japanese cucumbers can be dried without peeling.

2. Using a mandoline, slice the cucumbers into ¼-inch-thick slices.

3. Arrange the cucumbers in a single layer on the dehydrator trays.

To Dehydrate

1. Dehydrate at 135°F for 6 to 8 hours.

2. When dried, the cucumbers should be papery and crisp.

To Store

Dried cucumber slices stored in vacuum-sealed glass jars, or Mylar bags with oxygen absorbers, will keep for up to 2 years.

ELEVATE YOUR DISH: Rehydrate the dried cucumber slices in pickle juice left over from a jar of your favorite pickles. Place ½ cup dehydrated cucumber slices in a Mason jar. Add ½ cup pickle juice and cover with a lid. Leave the jar in the refrigerator overnight. You'll have fresh pickles to enjoy in the morning.

Eggplant

Prep time: 20 minutes / **Dehydration time:** 8 to 10 hours
Yield: ½ medium eggplant = 1 cup dehydrated = 1½ cups rehydrated

Eggplant is a versatile vegetable with a meaty texture that absorbs flavors easily. It works especially well in tomato dishes, curries, and Middle Eastern–inspired dishes. Choose small, firm eggplants that yield slightly to pressure. They should have glossy purple skin. Smaller eggplants are more tender—and less bitter.

To Prepare

1. Wash the eggplant in cold water.

2. Peel the eggplant and discard the peel. Dice the eggplant into ½-inch pieces or slice into ¼-inch rounds or strips. Place the diced eggplant in a bowl. Spritz the cut eggplant with lemon juice or ascorbic acid solution (page 23) to halt browning.

3. Arrange the eggplant in a single layer on the dehydrator trays.

To Dehydrate

1. Dehydrate at 135°F for 4 hours. Reduce the temperature to 125°F and continue drying for 4 to 6 hours.

2. When dried, the eggplant should be leathery and hard.

To Store

Dried eggplant stored in vacuum-sealed glass jars, or Mylar bags with oxygen absorbers, will keep for up to 2 years.

ELEVATE YOUR DISH: Dehydrated eggplant can be rehydrated with marinades and then grilled or fried. The eggplant soaks up marinade flavors like a sponge. Cooked, rehydrated eggplant has a chewy, meaty texture.

Greens

Prep time: 15 minutes / **Dehydration time:** 6 to 8 hours
Yield: 2 cups fresh greens = 1 cup dried = 1½ cups rehydrated

Sorrel, mustard greens, spinach, and other leafy greens add nutrition and flavor to soups, stews, and rice dishes. Choose crisp, unwilted leaves with good green color.

To Prepare

1. Wash the leafy greens in cold water. Pat them dry.

2. Smaller leaves may be left whole. Cut larger leaves into ¼-inch strips, chiffonade-style, as follows: Stack 3 to 5 leaves on top of each other. Place the stack of greens on a cutting board with a long side toward you. Beginning at the long side of the leaves, roll the stack together to form a tight roll. Slice the roll of greens into ¼-inch strips.

3. Arrange the strips of leafy greens in a thin layer on the dehydrator trays. The leaves will shrink as they dry.

To Dehydrate

1. Dehydrate at 125°F for 6 to 8 hours. After 4 hours, stir the greens to dry them faster and more evenly.

2. When dried, the greens should be crisp and brittle.

To Store

Dried greens stored in vacuum-sealed glass jars or Mylar bags with oxygen absorbers, will keep for up to 7 years.

MIX IT UP: Powder dehydrated leafy greens, spinach, lettuce, or kale in a blender to make a homemade greens supplement. Any edible greens can be used, but avoid using bitter-flavored greens, such as dandelion greens. Add 1 teaspoon to your morning smoothie for an added nutritional boost!

Kale & Collards

Prep time: 15 minutes / **Dehydration time:** 6 to 8 hours
Yield: 2 cups fresh kale = 1 cup dried = 2 cups rehydrated

Kale is a superfood rich in vitamins and antioxidants. Choose kale or collard leaves that are no more than 8 inches in length, with deep-green or red coloring. Lacinato, Russian red, redbor, and other flat-leafed kale are the best varieties to use for dehydrating. Kale and collards are richer in flavor in the fall and winter.

To Prepare

1. Wash kale or collard green leaves in cold water. Drain.

2. Cut the leaves chiffonade-style: Using a sharp knife, cut out the large center rib from each leaf, and discard it. Stack about 5 leaves, and roll them lengthwise into a tight roll. Cut in ¼-inch ribbons across the roll. Repeat with the remaining leaves.

3. Steam the prepared leaves by placing them in a covered steam basket over a pot of boiling water for 2 minutes. When the leaves are blanched, their color will brighten.

4. Chill the blanched strips of kale in ice water. Drain.

5. Arrange the prepared strips in a thin mound on the dehydrator trays. The leaves will shrink as they dry.

To Dehydrate

1. Dehydrate at 135°F for 6 to 8 hours. After 4 hours, stir the leaves, exposing any spots that are still moist.

2. When dried, the kale should be papery and brittle.

To Store

Dried kale or collards stored in vacuum-sealed glass jars, or Mylar bags with oxygen absorbers, will keep for up to 7 years.

Lettuce

Prep time: 5 minutes / **Dehydration time:** 6 to 8 hours
Yield: 1 head romaine lettuce = ¼ cup dried

Dehydrated lettuce can be added to smoothies, or powdered in a blender and used in muffins, bread, and other baked goods to amp up the nutrition. Lettuce dehydrates quickly. Green and red leaf lettuces, romaine lettuce, and butterhead lettuce are the best for dehydrating. (Iceberg lettuce does not dehydrate well.) For the best flavor, choose well-formed, tender leaves with no bitterness. Lettuce is not generally rehydrated.

To Prepare

1. Remove the coarse outer leaves from the lettuce and discard them. Wash the lettuce under cold, running water to remove grit and any insects. Cut off the lettuce core and separate the leaves. Drain the leaves.

2. Cut the leaves into fine, ¼-inch strips, chiffonade-style, as follows: Stack 3 to 5 leaves on top of each other. Place the stack of lettuce on a cutting board with a long side toward you. Beginning at the long side of the leaves, roll the stack together to form a tight roll. Slice the roll of lettuce into ¼-inch strips.

3. Arrange the ribbons of lettuce in a thin layer on the dehydrator trays. The leaves will shrink as they dry.

To Dehydrate

1. Dehydrate at 125°F for 6 to 8 hours. Stir the lettuce on the trays after 4 hours to expose more surface area on the leaves.

2. The lettuce is done when it is crisp and brittle.

To Store

Dried lettuce stored in vacuum-sealed glass jars, or Mylar bags with oxygen absorbers, will keep for up to 7 years.

Mushrooms

Prep time: 10 minutes / **Dehydration time:** 4 to 8 hours
Yield: 1 cup fresh mushrooms = ½ cup dried

Mushrooms add both protein and depth of flavor to soups, stews, sauces, and egg dishes. Only use store-bought mushrooms or foraged mushrooms that you know for certain are safe and edible. (The drying process does not remove toxins!)

To Prepare

1. Brush the mushrooms with a soft brush to remove any soil or debris. If the mushrooms are very dirty, wash them in cold water. Gently pat them dry with a paper towel.

2. Cut the mushrooms crosswise into ¼-inch slices. If the stems are woody, set them aside and dry them whole to process into a mushroom powder (see the Mix It Up tip).

3. Arrange the mushroom slices in a single layer on the dehydrator trays.

To Dehydrate

1. Dehydrate at 125°F for 4 to 8 hours.

2. When dried, the mushrooms should be crisp and brittle.

To Store

Dried mushrooms stored in vacuum-sealed glass jars, or in Mylar bags with oxygen absorbers, will keep for up to 5 years.

MIX IT UP: Dried mushrooms or dried mushroom stalks may be powdered. Mushroom powder can add flavor to gravy, soups, rubs, and marinades. To powder the dried mushrooms, place them in a blender and pulse until all the mushroom pieces are processed to a fine powder.

Onions

Prep time: 15 minutes / **Dehydration time:** 10 to 12 hours
Yield: 1 pound onions = 1½ cups dried = 2 cups rehydrated

Many types of onions are suitable for dehydrating including both sweet onions (like Walla Walla and Vidalia), and pungent onions (like yellow globe, Spanish, red, and white onions). For dehydrating, choose firm, heavy, round onions with clean, papery skin.

To Prepare

1. Cut a thin layer of onion from both the top and the bottom. Peel the onion. Discard the peel, the top, and the bottom portions of the onion.

2. Cut the onion in half lengthwise, from the top to the bottom. Using a mandoline, slice each half of the onion into ⅛-inch slices. Separate the onion pieces so they can dry faster.

3. Arrange the onion pieces in a thin layer on the dehydrator trays. The onions will shrink as they dry.

To Dehydrate

1. Dehydrate at 145°F for 4 hours. Reduce the temperature to 125°F and continue drying for 6 to 8 hours.

2. When dried, the onions should be leathery and brittle.

To Store

Dried onions stored in vacuum-sealed glass jars, or in Mylar bags with oxygen absorbers, will keep for up to 7 years.

ELEVATE YOUR DISH: Pungent onions gain a sweeter, more complex flavor when they are caramelized before dehydrating. To caramelize, sauté the sliced onions with ¾ cup water in a heavy-bottomed sauté pan over medium-high heat. Add more water as needed to keep the onions from sticking to the bottom of the pan. Continue stirring until the onions soften and turn golden brown, about 25 minutes.

Peppers (Hot & Sweet)

Prep time: 5 minutes / **Dehydration time:** 8 to 10 hours
Yield: 2 cups chopped peppers = 1 cup dried = 1½ cups rehydrated

Dehydrated peppers can be used in soups, sauces, stews, and added to egg dishes and casseroles. For the best flavor, choose firm, heavy peppers that are fully ripe. Wear gloves when working with hot peppers!

To Prepare

1. Wash the peppers in cold water.

2. Hold the stem upright with the base firmly on a cutting board. Slice down the sides of the pepper, from the stem to the base to remove the flesh from the core. Discard the stem, core, and seeds.

3. Slice the pepper pieces into ¼-inch strips or dice them into ¼-inch pieces.

4. Arrange the prepared peppers in a thin layer on a lined dehydrator tray.

To Dehydrate

1. Dehydrate at 135°F for 4 hours. Reduce the temperature to 125°F and continue drying for 4 to 6 hours.

2. When dried, the peppers should be hard and brittle.

To Store

Dried peppers stored in vacuum-sealed glass jars, or in Mylar bags with oxygen absorbers, will keep for up to 10 years.

ELEVATE YOUR DISH: Try smoking your peppers before dehydrating to add a great smoky flavor to your barbecue rubs and sauces. Turn up the heat by smoking jalapeño and other hot peppers before you dehydrate them. Red jalapeño peppers are smoked for chipotle seasoning in Mexican-inspired dishes (see the Mix It Up tip on page 85).

Potatoes

Prep and cook time: 45 minutes / **Dehydration time:** 10 to 12 hours
Yield: 4 medium potatoes = 1 cup dried = 1¼ cups rehydrated

Shredded, mashed, or sliced potatoes are a versatile addition to your pantry. Prepare them in several ways to expand your options during meal preparation. Yukon Gold, red Burbank, and russet potatoes are equally good for dehydrating. Choose full-size, young potatoes with thin skins for the best flavor and texture.

To Prepare

1. Wash the potatoes in cold water and scrub the skins with a firm brush. Peeling is optional.

2. Cook the potatoes in boiling water until they are tender when pierced with a fork, about 6 minutes. Remove from the heat and rinse in cold water to stop the cooking process.

3. Cut the potatoes into the form you plan to use them in, for instance, sliced potatoes for scalloped potatoes, diced potatoes for future soups, or shredded for hash browns. Pieces should be no more than ¼ inch thick.

4. Dip the potatoes in ascorbic acid solution to prevent browning. Drain the potatoes.

5. Arrange the prepared potatoes in a single layer on the dehydrator trays.

To Dehydrate

1. Dehydrate at 135°F for 4 hours. Reduce the temperature to 125°F and continue drying for 6 to 8 hours.

2. When dried, the potatoes should be hard.

To Store

Dried potatoes stored in vacuum-sealed glass jars, or in Mylar bags with oxygen absorbers, will keep for up to 5 years.

Summer Squash & Zucchini

Prep time: 15 minutes / **Dehydration time:** 12 to 14 hours
Yield: 2 medium zucchini = ½ cup dried = 1 cup rehydrated

Mild-flavored zucchini and summer squash add texture and bulk to soups, stews, and sauces. Choose well-formed, unblemished zucchini or summer squash of any size. Smaller Costata Romanesco zucchini have a nutty flavor and create attractive, scalloped-edge slices.

To Prepare

1. Wash the zucchini in cold water. If the zucchini has a hard skin, peel it. If the skin can be dented with a fingernail, there is no need to peel it.

2. Using a sharp knife, remove the stem and bottom ends of the squash. Cut larger zucchini in half, lengthwise. Remove the seeds and the spongy pulp. Smaller zucchini and summer squash can be left whole, minus the stem and bottom ends.

3. Slice smaller zucchini into ¼-inch slices or cubes. Shred larger zucchini in a food processor or with a box grater.

4. Arrange the slices or dice in a single layer on the dehydrator trays. Mound shredded zucchini in a thin layer on the dehydrator trays.

To Dehydrate

1. Dehydrate at 135°F for 4 hours. Reduce the temperature to 125°F and continue drying for 8 to 10 hours.

2. When dried, the zucchini and summer squash should be leathery and crisp.

To Store

Dried zucchini or summer squash stored in vacuum-sealed glass jars, or in Mylar bags with oxygen absorbers, will keep for up to 5 years.

Sweet Potatoes & Yams

Prep and cook time: 1 hour / **Dehydration time:** 10 to 12 hours
Yield: 2 cups fresh sweet potatoes = 1 cup dried = 1½ cups rehydrated

Sweet potatoes can be used interchangeably in recipes that call for pumpkin or winter squash. Choose firm, unblemished sweet potatoes and yams with copper-colored skin and deep-orange flesh. Leave the skin on for increased nutrition and fiber or peel them before blanching for a smoother texture.

To Prepare

1. Scrub the sweet potato skins with a vegetable brush under cold, running water until clean. Optionally, peel the sweet potatoes to reduce the fiber.

2. Cut into ¼-inch slices. Steam the sliced sweet potatoes for 5 minutes in a covered steam basket over a pot of boiling water, until they are cooked through. Sweet potatoes are cooked when a fork can easily be inserted without resistance.

3. Remove the sweet potatoes from the pot. Cool them to room temperature.

4. Arrange the cooked sweet potato slices in a single layer on the dehydrator trays.

To Dehydrate

1. Dehydrate at 145°F for 4 hours. Reduce the temperature to 135°F and continue drying for 6 to 8 hours.

2. When dried, the sweet potatoes should be hard and brittle.

To Store

Dried sweet potatoes or yams stored in vacuum-sealed glass jars, or in Mylar bags with oxygen absorbers, will keep for up to 5 years.

MIX IT UP: Try mashing the sweet potatoes before dehydrating them. Spread the mashed sweet potatoes on a fruit leather sheet and dry at 145°F for 8 to 10 hours until they are brittle. Powder the dried sweet potatoes in a blender. Use the sweet potato powder in place of pumpkin puree in soups, pies, and other baked goods.

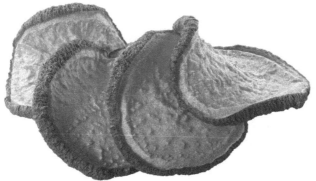

Tomatoes

Prep time: 10 minutes / **Dehydration time:** 8 to 10 hours
Yield: 1 pound tomatoes = 1 cup dried = 1½ cups rehydrated

Sun-dried tomatoes are a must for Mediterranean cooking. All tomatoes can be dehydrated in the same way, but meatier Roma tomatoes dehydrate faster and offer a plumper dried tomato. San Marzano tomatoes are traditionally used for Italian sun-dried tomatoes. For the best flavor and texture, choose firm, fully ripe tomatoes.

To Prepare

1. Wash the tomatoes in cold water. Pat them dry with a paper towel.

2. Using a sharp knife, slice the tomatoes lengthwise into ¼-inch slices.

3. Arrange the tomato slices in a single layer on the dehydrator trays.

To Dehydrate

1. Dehydrate at 140°F for 4 hours. Reduce the temperature to 130°F and continue drying for 4 to 6 hours.

2. When dried, the tomatoes should be leathery and crisp, with no soft spots.

To Store

Dried tomatoes stored in vacuum-sealed Mason jars, or in Mylar bags with oxygen absorbers, will keep for up to 5 years.

MIX IT UP: Using a blender, turn the dried tomatoes into tomato powder. Pulse until the tomatoes are reduced to a uniform powder. Use the tomato powder to thicken marinara sauce or anywhere you would normally use tomato paste.

Winter Squash & Pumpkins

Prep and cook time: 1 hour / **Dehydration time:** 10 to 12 hours
Yield: 1 (3-pound) winter squash = 1 cup dried = 2 cups rehydrated

Dehydrated pumpkins and winter squash may be used for desserts, vegetable sides, and hearty soups. Use them interchangeably for most recipes that call for pumpkin or squash. Choose thick-fleshed pie pumpkins or meaty winter squash like butternut, Hubbard, or kabocha squash for the sweetest flavor and best texture.

To Prepare

1. Cut the squash or pumpkin in half lengthwise. Scoop out the seeds and the stringy membrane.

2. Place the halves on a baking sheet. Bake the squash in a 350°F oven for 45 minutes, or until tender. Remove from the oven. Cool the squash until it can safely be handled.

3. Separate the soft flesh from the peel using a paring knife or large spoon. Cut the winter squash flesh into 1-inch cubes. Place the squash cubes in a blender and process on high to puree it. You should end up with 3 cups of puree.

4. Line dehydrator trays with fruit leather sheets or plastic wrap. Spread the pureed squash in an even layer over the dehydrator trays.

To Dehydrate

1. Dehydrate at 145°F for 4 hours. Reduce the temperature to 130°F and continue drying for 6 to 8 hours.

2. When dried, the winter squash should be leathery and brittle.

To Store

Dried winter squash or pumpkins stored in vacuum-sealed glass jars, or in Mylar bags with oxygen absorbers, will keep for up to 5 years.

MIX IT UP: Dehydrated pumpkin or squash can be powdered and used in soups or baking recipes for added nutrition. Place the dehydrated squash in a blender and puree to a uniform powder. If the squash is not dry enough, return the powdered squash to the lined dehydrator tray and dry for an additional 2 to 4 hours. Cool the powder before packaging it for storage.

CHAPTER 5

Dehydrating Herbs & Spices

R ich in antioxidants, vitamins, and minerals, herbs and spices are some of our most nutrient-dense foods. Dehydrating intensifies their flavors and aroma. Aromatic molecules in herbs offer both flavor and health benefits supporting healthy digestion, immunity, and circulation, as well as aiding relaxation. However, aromatic molecules are easily evaporated from the plant materials, so herbs and spices must be handled gently and dried at low temperatures to preserve their fragrance and flavor.

Sort herbs by removing dead leaves or discolored plant material. Rinse in cool water to remove dust and any insects that may be lurking in the plants. Pat the herbs dry with a kitchen towel. Place the individual leaves on the dehydrator trays and dry at 105°F for 4 to 6 hours. Remove the herbs from the dehydrator as soon as it's showing signs of being done—overdrying can lead to flavor loss.

You'll want to freeze spices like dill seed or lovage seed for 48 hours prior to dehydrating, to kill any stray insect eggs hiding in the seed. When drying roots such as horseradish, ginger, or turmeric, cut them into uniform slices and allow more time to dehydrate.

Although herbs and spices can be dried together, drying herbs separately from other foods will preserve their flavor and aroma. The heat necessary to dry other foods can cause damage to the delicate nature of herbs.

Herbs and spices are some of the most versatile dehydrated ingredients. Dried herbs and spices can be used as flavorings in your home-cooked meals. Combine dried herbs with aromatic vegetables to create traditional spice blends.

Create unique condiments from fresh garden herbs, like stevia, an herb that's sweeter than sugar, or chipotle peppers, with their smoky heat. Use your creativity to make health-supporting herbal tea from your dried herbs and spices. Aromatic leaves and flowers can fill your teacup with refreshing and energizing beverages all winter long, when you dry the herbs at their peak of readiness.

Anise, Fennel & Dill Seed

Prep time: 10 minutes / **Dehydration time:** 4 to 6 hours
Yield: 1 cup seeds = 1 cup dehydrated

Anise, fennel, and dill seed offer a mild licorice flavor to sauces, meat dishes, and vegetable sides. In many cuisines, they are eaten at the end of a meal to support healthy digestion and freshen your breath. These spices can be found in the grocery store already dried, but you can also dry the mature seeds from your own plants.

To Prepare

1. Remove the seeds from the anise, fennel, or dill plants. Clean the seed of any chaff and bits of branches by sifting the seeds through a coarse strainer.

2. Sift the seeds a second time through a fine strainer to remove more of the chaff and dust.

3. Line the dehydrator trays with fruit leather sheets.

4. Arrange the seeds in a thin pile on the dehydrator trays.

To Dehydrate

1. Dehydrate at 105°F for 4 to 6 hours.

2. When dried, the anise, fennel, and dill seed should be dry and brittle.

To Store

Anise, fennel, or dill seed stored in an airtight spice jar will last 1 to 2 years.

MIX IT UP: Anise, fennel, and dill seed offer digestive support that reduces stomach spasms and eases flatulence. Add 1 tablespoon of the seeds to bean or cabbage dishes in the last hour of cooking to reduce the discomfort these foods can cause.

Chipotle Peppers &
Smoked Paprika

Prep time: 10 minutes, plus 3 hours to smoke / **Dehydration time:** 10 hours
Yield: 2 cups fresh peppers = 1 cup dried = 4 teaspoons powdered

Chipotle peppers are ripe jalapeño peppers that are smoked before drying. When ripe peppers are smoked, the sugars in the peppers caramelize, adding earthy and fruity flavors. Smoked paprika uses the same technique but begins with ripe sweet peppers. Choose fully ripe red jalapeños, or red bell peppers that are firm and juicy to make smoked peppers. Don't forget to wear disposable gloves when working with hot peppers!

To Prepare

1. Wash the peppers, and remove the stems. Cut the peppers in half. Cut the larger peppers in quarters to make them easier to work with. Remove the seeds.

2. Place the prepared peppers in a grilling basket, in a single layer. Place the grilling basket in a wood-fired barbeque or smoker. Use the smoker or grill according to the manufacturer's directions.

3. Smoke the peppers at 225°F for 3 hours. The peppers will deepen in color but should not be black. If they seem to be blackening, raise them higher above the heat source.

4. Using tongs, remove the smoked peppers from the grill or smoker.

5. Arrange the peppers in a single layer, cut-side up, on the dehydrator trays.

To Dehydrate

1. Dehydrate at 125°F for 10 hours.

2. When dried, the peppers should be a rich, deep-red color, and leathery and hard.

To Store

Dried, smoked peppers stored in vacuum-sealed glass jars will keep for up to 5 years.

MIX IT UP: Chipotle peppers are traditionally made with red jalapeño peppers, but any fully ripe pepper can be smoked. Poblano peppers have about half the heat of jalapeños, and habanero peppers may be more than 100 times hotter than a mild jalapeño. Choose the peppers with the heat level you prefer.

Citrus Zest

Prep time: 5 minutes / **Dehydration time:** 4 hours
Yield: 2 tablespoons fresh citrus zest = 2 teaspoons dried

Citrus zest brightens the flavor of cookies, cakes, poultry and fish dishes, and herbal tea. It's easy to make it at home anytime you have citrus fruit. Choose juicy, fragrant, organic lemons, oranges, limes, or other citrus fruit with a deeply colored peel.

To Prepare

1. Wash the citrus in cold water with a squirt of dish soap and vinegar. Soak briefly to remove grime and pesticide residues, then rinse and pat dry.

2. Using a citrus zester or a grater, remove a thin layer of peel from citrus fruit. Take as little of the bitter white pith with the peel as possible. Rotate the fruit in your hand as you remove the zest.

3. Line a dehydrator tray with a fruit leather sheet.

4. Arrange the citrus zest in a thin layer on the lined dehydrator tray.

To Dehydrate

1. Dehydrate at 105°F for 4 hours.

2. When dried, the citrus zest should be hard and brittle.

To Store

Dried citrus zest stored in vacuum-sealed glass jars will keep for up to 2 years.

ELEVATE YOUR DISH: Add a pinch of dried citrus zest to your herbal tea blends. It will brighten the flavor and elevate your mood.

Garlic

Prep time: 15 minutes / **Dehydration time:** 8 to 10 hours
Yield: 5 heads of garlic = ¼ cup dehydrated = ½ cup rehydrated

Once you've tasted your own homemade garlic powder, you will never be satisfied with store-bought garlic powder. Garlic releases its flavor, "allicin," when the garlic is crushed or cut. To get the fullest flavor, you'll want to cut, crush, or break the cloves before dehydrating. Choose firm, blemish-free garlic heads with uniform color on the papery wrappers.

To Prepare

1. Separate the garlic cloves from each head of garlic. Press each garlic clove firmly with the flat side of a chef's knife to break the papery peel. Peel the garlic cloves. Cut off the bottom of each clove, and slice them into ¼-inch slices using a sharp knife.

2. Line the dehydrator trays with fruit leather sheets or parchment paper.

3. Arrange the prepared garlic in a single layer on lined dehydrator trays.

To Dehydrate

1. Dehydrate at 135°F for 2 hours. Reduce the temperature to 115°F and continue drying for 6 to 8 hours.

2. When dried, the garlic should be hard and brittle.

To Store

Dried garlic stored in vacuum-sealed glass jars, or in Mylar bags with oxygen absorbers, will keep for up to 2 years.

ELEVATE YOUR DISH: Powder dehydrated garlic in a blender. Use it anywhere you would use garlic salt or garlic powder. Use it in garlic butter, salad dressings, marinara sauce, and Mediterranean recipes.

Ginger & Turmeric

Prep time: 30 minutes / **Dehydration time:** 6 to 8 hours
Yield: 1 (4-ounce) ginger root = ½ cup dried = ¾ cup rehydrated

Ginger and turmeric are essential ingredients in curries, herbal teas, and many Asian and Middle Eastern dishes, and are dried in the same way. Choose ginger and turmeric roots with thin, tight skin. If the skin is wrinkled, the ginger and turmeric are past their prime.

To Prepare

1. Wash the ginger or turmeric roots in cold water. Pat them dry.

2. Peel the ginger or turmeric roots by scraping them with the edge of a spoon.

3. Slice the peeled ginger or turmeric into ⅛-inch slices using a mandoline or a sharp knife.

4. Arrange the prepared ginger or turmeric in a single layer on the dehydrator trays.

To Dehydrate

1. Dehydrate at 110°F for 6 to 8 hours.

2. When dried, the ginger and turmeric should be leathery and pliable.

To Store

Dried ginger or turmeric stored in vacuum-sealed glass jars, or in Mylar bags with oxygen absorbers, will keep for up to 5 years.

ELEVATE YOUR DISH: Make an herbal tea blend to support healthy digestion and elevate your mood. Prepare as herbal tea by placing ½ teaspoon dehydrated ginger pieces, ½ teaspoon dehydrated turmeric pieces, and ½ teaspoon dehydrated lemon zest in your tea strainer. Add a twist of freshly ground black pepper to enhance the healthful properties of the tea.

Herbs for Tea (Mint, Lemon Balm, Lemongrass & Lemon Verbena)

Prep time: 15 minutes / **Dehydration time:** 4 to 6 hours
Yield: 2 cups fresh herbs = ½ cup dried

Herbs that are used for tea are rich in flavor and volatile oils that evaporate easily in high heat. To preserve their flavor and antioxidants, herbs are dried at a lower temperature. Use these herbs to make your favorite tea blends. Many of these herbs support healthy digestion and help you relax as well as offering delicious flavor. You can find these easy-to-grow herbs at the farmers' market; fresh lemongrass can be found at most Asian markets. For the most intense flavor, choose herbs with vibrant color.

To Prepare

1. Wash the herbs by submerging them in a bowl of cold water. Remove them from the water and drain them.

2. Strip the leaves from the stems of the mint, lemon balm, and lemon verbena by pinching the base of the stem and sliding your thumb and forefinger toward the tip of the stem, removing the leaves. Discard any damaged leaves. Cut the long leaves of lemongrass into ½-inch pieces. The leaves of other herbs can be left whole.

3. Arrange the herbs in a thin pile on the dehydrator trays. The leaves will shrink as they dry.

To Dehydrate

1. Dehydrate at 105°F for 4 to 6 hours.

2. When dried, the herbs should be crisp and crumble when squeezed in your hand.

To Store

Stored in vacuum-sealed glass jars, protected from light and heat, the dried tea herbs will last 2 to 3 years.

ELEVATE YOUR DISH: Make simple syrups using your dried herbs. These can be used in beverages and cocktails. Make a strong tea using ¼ cup dried herbs with 2 cups boiled water. Steep the herbs with a cover on for 15 minutes, then strain the spent herbs from the liquid. Stir 2 cups sugar into the tea until it dissolves. Transfer the mixture to an airtight container and keep refrigerated. This simple syrup will last 1 to 2 weeks in the refrigerator.

Horseradish

Prep time: 20 minutes / **Dehydration time:** 6 to 8 hours
Yield: ½ pound fresh horseradish root = ½ cup dried = ¾ cup rehydrated

Dried horseradish is not as pungent as freshly prepared horseradish, but it still has a bite. It is a flavorful condiment to serve with beef or pork that won't burn your sinuses. Choose fresh, firm horseradish roots with thin skin.

To Prepare

1. Wash the horseradish in cold water. Using a vegetable brush, brush the roots of the horseradish to remove any dirt.

2. Prepare the horseradish in a well-ventilated space. Using the flat edge of a paring knife, scrape the thin peel from the horseradish. Discard the peelings.

3. To prepare horseradish roots that are less than ½ inch thick, slice the root crossways into ¼-inch pieces. If your horseradish root is larger, shred it on the side of a box grater.

4. Line a dehydrator tray with a fruit leather sheet or parchment paper.

5. Arrange the prepared horseradish in a single layer on the lined dehydrator tray.

To Dehydrate

1. Dehydrate at 140°F for 1 hour. Reduce the temperature to 120°F and continue drying for 5 to 7 hours.

2. When dried, the horseradish should be hard and brittle.

To Store

Dried horseradish stored in vacuum-sealed glass jars will keep for up to 2 years.

Lovage

Prep time: 15 minutes / **Dehydration time:** 6 to 8 hours
Yield: 2 cups fresh lovage leaves = ½ cup dried

Lovage is a perennial herb with a flavor similar to celery. The leaves, seeds, and roots of this aromatic plant are used for flavoring poultry and fish dishes, soups, and casseroles. You may find lovage at your local farmers' market or specialty grocery stores. It is a common herb in southern European, German, and eastern European cuisines.

To Prepare

1. Wash the lovage by swishing the leaves in a sink of cold water. If you are preserving the root, scrub it with a vegetable brush to remove any dirt. Drain.

2. Remove any discolored leaves or leaves with insect damage. Cut the leaves or roots into 1-inch pieces.

3. Arrange the leaves in a single layer on a dehydrator tray. Arrange the lovage root in a single layer on a separate dehydrator tray.

To Dehydrate

1. Dehydrate at 105°F for 6 to 8 hours. The leaves should be dried in 6 hours. The root is thin and should be dried in 8 hours.

2. The lovage is done when the leaves or root are hard and brittle. The leaves will crumble easily.

To Store

Stored separately in vacuum-sealed glass jars, protected from light and heat, the lovage leaves and roots will keep for up to 2 years.

Mirepoix or Soffritto Spice Blends

Prep time: 20 minutes / **Dehydration time:** 8 to 10 hours
Yield: 2 cups vegetables = 1 cup dried = 1½ cups rehydrated

Mirepoix and soffritto are essential aromatic vegetable blends used as bases for soups, sauces, and stews. They are made up of finely cut onions, carrots, and celery.

1 large onion (yellow or red),
1 medium carrot
1 medium celery stalk, with leaves

To Prepare

1. Wash and peel the onion. Discard the peel. Dice the onion into ¼-inch pieces. Set aside in a bowl.

2. Wash and peel the carrot. Dice the carrot into ¼-inch cubes. Set aside in a separate bowl.

3. Wash the celery stalk. Cut the stalk lengthwise into 3 or 4 pieces. Finely chop the pieces into ¼-inch dice. Set aside in a separate bowl.

4. Line the dehydrator trays with the fruit leather sheets.

5. Arrange the onions, carrots, and celery in a single layer on separate dehydrator trays, as they have different densities and may be done at different times.

To Dehydrate

1. Dehydrate at 125°F for 8 to 10 hours. Remove the vegetables as they become fully dry.

2. When dried, the onions, carrots, and celery should be hard, crisp, and leathery.

3. Combine the dehydrated onions, carrots, and celery together in a bowl. Stir these together to make a uniform mixture.

To Store

Dried mirepoix stored in a vacuum-sealed glass jar will keep for up to 3 years.

Oregano, Basil & Thyme

Prep time: 10 minutes / **Dehydration time:** 4 hours
Yield: 1 cup fresh leaves = ¼ cup dried

Strongly aromatic herbs such as oregano, basil, and thyme are best when they are dried shortly after purchase, when the volatile oils are the strongest. Choose clean, deeply colored leaves with no wilting or yellowing. If you are picking from your own garden, harvest the stalks of herbs by cutting the stem above a two-leaf set. The plant will grow two new stalks where there once was one! Pick them after the dew dries in the morning but before the sun touches the plants, as it evaporates the volatile oils.

To Prepare

1. Do not wash the herbs. Discard damaged, dirty, or broken leaves from the stems. Strip the clean leaves from each stem by pinching the base of the stem and drawing up the stem with your fingers, from the base to the tip. The leaves will separate easily from the stem.

2. Arrange each type of herb in a single layer on a separate dehydrator tray. The leaves will shrink as they dry.

To Dehydrate

1. Dehydrate at 105°F for 4 hours.

2. When dried, the herbs should be crisp and crumbly.

To Store

Stored separately in vacuum-sealed glass jars, protected from light and heat, each herb will keep for 2 to 3 years.

Paprika

Prep time: 10 minutes / **Dehydration time:** 10 hours
Yield: 2 cups fresh peppers = 1 cup dried = 4 teaspoons powdered

Paprika is made from dried sweet peppers, bell peppers, or mild Hungarian peppers. It adds a pop of color, as well as a fruity spiciness to deviled eggs, potato salad, hummus, and goulash. Add it near the end of your cooking time to get the most flavor and color in your food. For the best flavor and color, choose ripe, red sweet peppers, with firm, juicy flesh.

To Prepare

1. Wash the peppers and remove the stems. Cut the peppers in quarters and remove the seeds. Dice the peppers into ¼-inch pieces.

2. Arrange the prepared peppers in a single layer on the dehydrator trays.

To Dehydrate

1. Dehydrate at 125°F for 10 hours.

2. When dried, the peppers should be leathery and hard with a rich, deep-red color.

To Store

Dried sweet peppers stored in vacuum-sealed glass jars will keep for up to 10 years. Powder the peppers in a blender to make paprika, just before you need it. Paprika powder will last for up to 3 months when stored out of light and heat.

MIX IT UP: Smoke the sweet peppers on a wood-fired grill or in a smoker to give them a fruity, earthy flavor before dehydrating. Smoking deepens the color and sweetens the flavor. (See the Mix It Up tip on page 85.)

Parsley & Cilantro

Prep time: 10 minutes / **Dehydration time:** 2 to 3 hours
Yield: 1 cup fresh parsley or cilantro = ½ cup dried

The leaves of parsley and cilantro are used in both cooked dishes and salads. Stronger-flavored flat-leaf parsley is best for dehydrating. The leaves of cilantro are dried in the same way as parsley. For either herb, choose a bunch with deeply colored green leaves with strong scent.

To Prepare

1. Wash the parsley or cilantro by swishing it in a bowl of cold water. Remove it from the water.

2. Place the cleaned leaves in the basket of a salad spinner. Spin them till most of the water is drained. The salad spinner allows you to dry the leaves without bruising them.

3. Remove the leaves from the stems. Discard any discolored or damaged leaves.

4. Arrange the whole leaves in a single layer on the dehydrator trays.

To Dehydrate

1. Dehydrate at 105°F for 2 to 3 hours.

2. When dried, the parsley or cilantro leaves should be crispy and brittle.

To Store

Dried parsley or cilantro stored in vacuum-sealed glass jars, protected from light and heat, will keep for 2 to 3 years in storage.

Rose Hips

Prep time: 30 minutes / **Dehydration time:** 3 to 6 hours
Yield: 1 cup fresh rose hips = ½ cup dried

Rose hips are the fruit of the rose plant. Rich in vitamin C, they are used in herbal tea for their citrusy flavor. Rose hips may be found in the fall at the farmers' market or some natural food markets. Choose firm red or orange rose hips, when their color is strong. If you are using the rose hips in tea, there is no need to remove the seeds. However, if you plan to use the rose hips for food, such as in rose hip soup, jam, or jelly, remove the seeds before drying.

To Prepare

1. Wash the rose hips and discard any that are damaged or discolored. Remove the stem and the bottom of each rose hip by pinching out the wiry hairs.

2. If using the rose hips for food, remove the seeds by cutting each rose hip in half. Using a small spoon or ¼ teaspoon measuring spoon, remove and discard the seeds from both halves of the rose hip.

3. Arrange the rose hips in a single layer, cut-side up, on the dehydrator trays.

To Dehydrate

1. Dehydrate at 100°F for 3 to 6 hours, to preserve their vitamin C content. Seeded rose hips will dry in 3 to 4 hours. Whole rose hips take longer to dry.

2. When dried, the rose hips should be hard and brittle.

To Store

Dried rose hips stored in vacuum-sealed Mason jars, protected from light and heat, will keep for up to 2 years. Their vitamin C content dissipates in storage, but their other antioxidants, such as lycopene, remain stable.

Sage

Prep time: 5 minutes / **Dehydration time:** 4 to 6 hours
Yield: 1 cup fresh sage leaves = ½ cup dried

A must for turkey dressing and chicken soup, sage leaves have a greasy feel, even after drying, due to the abundance of volatile oils on the leaf surface. If you grow your own, choose whole leaves or sprigs of sage, and harvest before the plant puts out flowers.

To Prepare

1. Do not wash the sage leaves. Remove the damaged, discolored, or soiled leaves. Separate the sage leaves from the stems.

2. Arrange the sage leaves in a single layer on the dehydrator trays.

To Dehydrate

1. Dehydrate at 105°F for 4 to 6 hours.

2. When dried, the sage leaves should be brittle and easily crumble when crushed.

To Store

Whole dried sage leaves stored in vacuum-sealed glass jars, protected from light and heat, will keep for up to 3 years.

ELEVATE YOUR DISH: Homemade poultry spice is fragrant and delicious. Add ¼ cup dried sage leaves, ½ cup dried parsley, ¼ cup dried thyme, and 2 tablespoons dried rosemary to a blender. Pulse on high until the herbs are powdered. Use in place of commercial spice in your poultry dressing.

Stevia

Prep time: 10 minutes / **Dehydration time:** 4 to 6 hours
Yield: 2 cups fresh stevia leaves = ½ cup dried = 2 tablespoons powder

Stevia is a calorie-free sugar substitute made from the leaves of the stevia plant (*Stevia rebaudiana*). It is 200 times sweeter than sugar. Purchase vibrantly colored stevia leaves at the farmers' market in the fall, when the cooler weather increases the sugar in the leaves. You may also find potted stevia plants in the produce section of your grocery store.

To Prepare

1. Wash the stevia leaves or stems by submerging them in a bowl of cold water. Remove them from the water and drain.

2. Strip the leaves from the stems by hand. Pinch the base of the stem and slide your thumb and forefinger toward the tip of the stem, removing the leaves. Discard any discolored or damaged leaves. Keep the stevia leaves whole.

3. Arrange the stevia leaves in a thin pile on the dehydrator trays. The leaves will shrink as they dry.

To Dehydrate

1. Dehydrate at 105°F for 4 to 6 hours.

2. When dried, the stevia leaves should be crispy and crumble when squeezed in your hand.

To Store

Dried stevia leaves stored in vacuum-sealed glass jars, protected from light and heat, will keep for 2 to 3 years.

ELEVATE YOUR DISH: Use a pinch of dried stevia in herbal tea to add sweetness, or powder it and use it in recipes in the place of sugar. A tablespoon of powdered, dried stevia leaf is about the same sweetness as 1 cup of refined sugar. When swapping stevia for the sugar, try substituting only half the sugar a recipe calls for so that the texture doesn't change radically.

CHAPTER 6

Dehydrating Meat & Fish

Dehydrated meat, poultry, and fish are a mainstay in camping and hiking meals. Lightweight and portable, they've been eaten by nomads, adventurers, and travelers for centuries. Today, dehydrated meat and jerky are praised as protein-rich snacks for all.

There are two types of dehydrated meats: jerky and dehydrated cooked meat, including poultry and fish. The drying process is similar for both. However, the preparation is unique for different kinds of animal protein foods.

Only lean meat, skinless poultry, and low-fat fish should be dried for long-term storage. Because fat goes rancid in storage, promoting rapid spoilage, you'll need to remove all visible fat that is present on the meat you plan to dehydrate. Fattier fish like salmon can be dehydrated, but it should be stored in the freezer after dehydrating and eaten within 6 months. Blot cooked meat with paper towels to remove excess oil.

Meat intended for dehydration should be braised or simmered in water until tender to cook it, before you dry it. Cube cooked meat into ½-inch pieces, and drain and chill before dehydrating. Spread the pieces evenly on the dehydrator trays and dehydrate at 145°F for 4 hours. Reduce the temperature to 130°F and continue drying until the meat is fully dry. While the meat is drying, continue to blot any beads of oil that might come up on the meat. Properly dried, cooked meat should be hard and dry throughout. Test it by cutting a piece in half—it should be difficult to cut!

Jerky, on the other hand, is generally not precooked before being dehydrated. Instead, it is cured in a brine solution or a dry rub. This cure reduces surface bacteria while adding flavor. Jerky is dehydrated at 165°F for at least 4 hours. This pasteurizes the meat and prevents spoilage. Finished jerky is pliable and leathery. It will crack if bent but will not break apart. You'll find specific instructions with each recipe.

If your dehydrator will not reach 165°F, use the highest temperature available to you and dry for at least 6 hours. Then pasteurize your dried jerky in a preheated oven at 275°F for 10 minutes.

Candied Salmon Jerky

Prep time: 30 minutes, plus 1 hour to chill / **Dehydration time:** 6 hours / **Yield:** 10 pieces

This is a prized West Coast food. You can find it at roadside stands, in grocery stores, and at farm stands in rural communities along the coast from Alaska to California. Candied salmon is traditionally made by brining and then smoking salmon pieces until they are dry and firm. This recipe uses liquid smoke instead of the traditional open fire pit.

2 pounds frozen
  salmon fillets

¼ cup sea salt

¼ cup brown sugar

2 tablespoons
  maple syrup

1 teaspoon liquid smoke

To Prepare

1. Pat the salmon dry with a paper towel. Lay the salmon fillets on a cutting board, skin-side down. Feel the fish with your hands, and using tweezers, remove any little bones you find. Discard the bones.

2. Cut the salmon lengthwise from head to tail into ½-inch strips. Cut each strip in half. Leave the skin on the fish because it helps hold it together. Place the fish in a large bowl.

3. In a small bowl, pour in the salt, brown sugar, maple syrup, and liquid smoke. Stir to combine well. Pour the brine mixture into the bowl with the fish.

4. Stir the fish around in the brine to coat all sides. Cover the bowl with plastic wrap and refrigerate for 1 hour.

5. Remove the bowl from the refrigerator. Drain the salmon pieces.

6. Arrange the salmon strips in a single layer on the dehydrator trays.

To Dehydrate

1. Dehydrate at 165°F for 6 hours.

2. When done, the salmon jerky should be leathery, firm, and chewy.

3. If your dehydrator doesn't get as hot as 165°F, use the highest temperature available to you. After the jerky is finished, place it on a paper-towel-lined baking sheet. Bake it in a preheated 275°F oven for 10 minutes to bring the internal temperature up to 165°F. Remove it from the oven. Use a paper towel to blot the surface of the jerky to remove any excess oil.

4. Cool the salmon jerky to room temperature before you package it.

To Store

Candied Salmon Jerky stored in a vacuum-sealed bag will last 2 to 3 weeks at room temperature, 3 to 6 months in the refrigerator, or up to a year in the freezer.

PREP LIKE A PRO: Wild sockeye salmon is the best fish to use for candied salmon; however, it may carry parasites. Freezing the salmon for 2 weeks prior to turning it into jerky ensures that these parasites are neutralized. Work with the salmon while there are still ice crystals remaining in the fish, to make the salmon easier to cut and to prevent bacterial contamination.

Chipotle Beef Jerky

Prep time: 30 minutes / **Dehydration time:** 4 to 6 hours / **Yield:** 15 pieces

Spicy and smoky, chipotle beef jerky has the sweet smokiness and the kick jerky lovers favor. This one gets its bite from smoked red jalapeño peppers. If it's not hot enough for you, add some hot sauce or more peppers to increase the fire. This recipe is made with ground beef.

1 pound lean ground beef

1 tablespoon ground
  chipotle peppers
  (page 85)

½ teaspoon ground cumin

½ teaspoon garlic powder

½ teaspoon paprika

½ teaspoon dried oregano
  (page 93)

½ teaspoon salt

To Prepare

1. Place the ground beef in a large bowl and break it up with a wooden spoon.

2. Sprinkle the ground peppers, cumin, garlic powder, paprika, oregano, and salt into the ground beef. Work it in with your hands to thoroughly blend the spices in with the meat.

3. Spoon the ground beef mixture into the tube of a jerky gun. Press the beef jerky out of the jerky gun directly onto the dehydrator trays. The jerky should be ½ inch wide in strips about 4 to 5 inches long. (Alternatively, place the prepared jerky mixture in a 1-quart freezer bag. Cut ¼ inch from the corner tip off. Press the jerky mixture through the opening in a smooth, straight strip about 4 inches long.)

To Dehydrate

1. Dehydrate at 165°F for 4 to 6 hours. The jerky is done when it is hard and brittle, with no moist areas in the center of the jerky.

2. If your dehydrator doesn't get as hot as 165°F, use the highest temperature available to you. After the jerky is finished, place it on a paper-towel-lined baking sheet. Bake it in a preheated 275°F oven for 10 minutes to bring the internal temperature up to 165°F. Remove it from the oven. Use a paper towel to blot the surface of the jerky and remove any excess oil.

3. Cool the beef jerky to room temperature before you package it.

To Store

Chipotle Beef Jerky stored in a vacuum-sealed bag will last 2 to 3 weeks at room temperature, 3 to 5 months in the refrigerator, or up to a year in the freezer.

ELEVATE YOUR DISH: Sweeten the jerky by adding 1 tablespoon of honey or maple syrup when you add the spices. The additional sweetness contrasts well with the spiciness of the smoked peppers.

Cranberry Turkey Jerky

Prep time: 30 minutes / **Dehydration time:** 6 hours / **Yield:** 30 pieces

Cranberry turkey jerky echoes the delicious flavors of a holiday dinner: sage, cranberries, turkey, and stuffing. Choose fresh, lean, ground turkey with no more than 7 percent fat, and keep it frozen until you are ready to make the jerky. You'll want to thaw it in the refrigerator the night before you plan to dehydrate it. (It's easiest to work with if there are a few remaining ice crystals in the meat.)

2 pounds ground turkey

½ cup dried cranberries (page 41)

1 teaspoon dried onions, crushed (page 75)

2 tablespoons honey

½ teaspoon dried sage, crushed (page 97)

½ teaspoon sea salt

½ teaspoon freshly ground black pepper

To Prepare

1. Thaw the ground turkey in the refrigerator for several hours or overnight. Transfer the turkey to a large bowl.

2. In a blender, powder the dried cranberries and transfer to a small bowl. Add the onions, honey, sage, salt, and pepper. Stir the mixture to fully combine. Add the spice mixture to the bowl with the turkey.

3. With a spatula, mix the ground turkey with the cranberry mixture to make a uniform dough.

4. Spoon the ground turkey dough into the tube of a jerky gun. Press the dough out of the jerky gun directly onto the dehydrator trays. The jerky should be ½ inch wide in strips about 4 to 5 inches long. Place these close together on the dehydrator trays. Repeat until all of the turkey jerky dough is used up.

To Dehydrate

1. Dehydrate at 165°F for 6 hours or until the jerky is leathery and hard.

2. When dried, the jerky should be a hard stick with no soft spots in the middle.

3. If your dehydrator doesn't get as hot as 165°F, use the highest temperature available to you. After the jerky is finished, place it on a paper-towel-lined baking sheet. Bake it in a preheated 275°F oven for 10 minutes to bring the internal temperature up to 165°F. Remove it from the oven. Use a paper towel to blot the surface of the jerky and remove any excess oil.

4. Cool the turkey jerky to room temperature before you package it.

To Store

Cranberry Turkey Jerky stored in a vacuum-sealed bag will last 2 to 3 weeks at room temperature, 3 to 6 months in the refrigerator, or up to a year in the freezer.

PREP LIKE A PRO: If you do not have a jerky gun, you can use a freezer bag. Spoon the jerky mixture into the freezer bag. Cut one bottom corner of the freezer bag, removing about ¼ inch from the point. Fold down the top of the bag to put pressure on the jerky mixture. The turkey jerky dough will push through the cut-off corner into a ½-inch round strip.

Fajita Beef

Prep and cook time: 20 minutes / **Dehydration time:** 7 hours
Yield: 1 cup dried beef = 1½ cups rehydrated

Dried, cooked ground beef is a convenient pantry staple that's perfect for grab-and-go lunches, or weeknights when you're crunched for time. But dehydrated ground beef has a bad reputation. Some call it "backpacker's gravel" because it's notoriously difficult to rehydrate. To compensate, I add a starchy ingredient to draw water into the rehydrating meat, to soften it more quickly. This recipe uses breadcrumbs as the starchy ingredient. Fajita beef tastes delicious in nachos, tacos, or wraps.

1 pound lean ground beef

¼ cup dried sweet peppers (page 76)

¼ cup dried onions (page 75)

2 cloves garlic, peeled and crushed

1 teaspoon chili powder

2 teaspoons ground chipotle peppers (page 85)

½ cup breadcrumbs (use gluten-free if desired)

¼ cup water

To Prepare

1. In a large bowl, place the ground beef. Break up the sweet peppers and onions by crushing them in your hands, and add them to the bowl with the ground beef. Add the garlic, chili powder, chipotle peppers, and breadcrumbs. Mix it all together with your hands.

2. Heat the water in a medium skillet over medium heat. Add the beef mixture and break it apart with a spatula. Fry until the beef is browned and no pink remains in the meat. Turn the meat often to prevent it from over-browning.

3. Transfer the cooked beef mixture to a metal colander. Drain the meat.

4. Transfer the beef to dehydrator trays lined with mesh screens. Spread the meat into a thin layer. Using your fingers, break apart any large pieces so that the mixture dries evenly.

To Dehydrate

1. Dehydrate at 145°F for 7 hours.

2. When dried, the meat should be hard and brittle.

To Store

Dried beef stored in a vacuum-sealed bag with an oxygen absorber will last one year, if kept in a cool, dry place, protected from light.

PREP LIKE A PRO: Other lean ground meats can be dehydrated in a similar way to beef. Add ½ cup breadcrumbs, tapioca starch, potato starch, or rice flour to each pound of raw ground meat. Mix it well. Fry it in water rather than oil, to avoid any added fat, which can decrease its shelf life.

Ginger Beef Jerky

Prep time: 15 minutes, plus 45 minutes to chill / **Dehydration time:** 6 to 8 hours / **Yield:** 16 pieces

Almost every beef jerky recipe relies on soy sauce or tamari to give it its salty, umami flavor. In this recipe, ginger and garlic pair well with tamari and elevate this simple jerky recipe. This comes together so easily; you can make it tonight and pack it into lunch boxes in the morning! The best beef for jerky is lean, without a lot of fat marbling in the meat. Fat can spoil and shorten the storage life of your jerky. Cuts like sirloin, round, chuck, rump, or flank steaks are inexpensive and make the best jerky.

1 pound lean beef

½ cup gluten-free tamari

¼ cup red wine

¼ cup apple cider vinegar

1 tablespoon honey

1 tablespoon Dijon mustard

1 tablespoon dried onions, crushed

2 garlic cloves, peeled, minced

1 tablespoon powdered ginger

½ teaspoon cumin

½ teaspoon freshly ground black pepper

To Prepare

1. Trim any visible fat from the beef. Remove any silver sinew on the surface of the meat and discard it. Slice the beef into ¼-inch strips. Slicing with the grain will make a chewier jerky; jerky that is sliced against the grain is more tender and brittle. Set the strips of meat aside while you make the marinade.

2. In a 2-quart container, pour in the tamari, wine, vinegar, honey, mustard, onions, garlic, ginger, cumin, and pepper. Whisk the marinade briefly to combine well.

3. Add the strips of meat, pressing them down to submerge them in the marinade.

4. Cover the container and refrigerate it for 45 minutes.

5. Drain the jerky from the marinade.

6. Arrange the jerky in a single layer on the dehydrator trays.

To Dehydrate

1. Dehydrate at 165°F for 6 to 8 hours. The jerky is done when it is leathery and firm, but still pliable. Test the jerky's doneness when it is cooled. It should bend but not snap when it is done.

2. If your dehydrator doesn't get as hot as 165°F, use the highest temperature available to you. After the jerky is finished, place it on a paper-towel-lined baking sheet. Bake it in a preheated 275°F oven for 10 minutes to bring the internal temperature up to 165°F. Remove it from the oven. Use a paper towel to blot the surface of the jerky and remove any excess oil.

3. Cool the jerky to room temperature before you package it.

To Store

Ginger Beef Jerky stored in a vacuum-sealed bag will last 2 to 3 weeks at room temperature, 3 to 6 months in the refrigerator, or up to a year in the freezer.

ELEVATE YOUR DISH: Add smoky flavor to the jerky by adding 1 tablespoon of liquid smoke or smoked paprika (see the Mix It Up tip on page 94) to the marinade.

Ham Cubes

Prep time: 15 minutes / **Dehydration time:** 8 hours
Yield: 3 cups dried ham = 5 cups rehydrated

Dehydrated ham is useful to keep in the pantry for weeknight meals. Ham pairs well with macaroni and cheese, hash browns, and rice dishes. Dehydrated ham can be added to strongly flavored soups to add a salty sweetness and a toothsome texture. Choose lean, cooked ham for dehydrating. Trim off any visible fat, as it can cause the meat to spoil prematurely.

---

2 pounds lean ham, precooked

To Prepare

1. Trim any visible fat from the ham. Cut the ham into ¼-inch cubes.

2. Line the dehydrator trays with mesh screens.

3. Arrange the cubed ham in a single layer on the dehydrator trays.

To Dehydrate

1. Dehydrate at 145°F for 4 hours. Reduce the temperature to 135°F and continue drying for 4 hours.

2. Blot the meat periodically with a paper towel to remove any visible fat beads on the surface of the meat.

3. When dried, the ham should be hard and firm.

To Store

Dried ham stored in vacuum-sealed bags will last for a year in the freezer.

PREP LIKE A PRO: Any leftover ham can be used for dehydrating, but you can save time by starting with deli ham sandwich meat. Have the deli slice it into thick, ¼-inch slices. Trim off the visible fat at home. It can be dried in strips for jerky or cubed and dehydrated according to this recipe.

Lemon Pepper Fish Jerky

Prep time: 30 minutes, plus 4 hours to chill / **Dehydration time:** 6 to 8 hours / **Yield:** 30 pieces

Fish used for dehydrating should be freshly caught or flash-frozen immediately after being caught. Fish begins to deteriorate as soon as it leaves the water. One way to tell if it's good? Fresh fish does not smell "fishy." Keep frozen fish in the freezer until you are ready to work with it. For the best results, choose low-fat fillets of cod, haddock, pollock, or sole.

2 pounds whitefish fillets, such as cod, haddock, or sole

Juice and grated zest of 1 lemon

2 tablespoons distilled white vinegar

1 tablespoon freshly ground black pepper

1 teaspoon sea salt

1 teaspoon onion powder (page 75)

1 tablespoon dried parsley (page 95)

To Prepare

1. Rinse the fish fillets in cold water. Pat them dry with a paper towel.

2. Slice the fillets into ¼-inch slices across the grain. Refrigerate the fish slices while you make the marinade.

3. In a 2-quart container with a lid, combine the lemon juice and zest, vinegar, pepper, salt, onion powder, and parsley. Mix well.

4. Add the sliced fish to the container. Press down on the fish slices to submerge them in the marinade. Cover the marinade container and refrigerate for 4 hours.

5. Remove the fish from the marinade and drain in a colander.

6. Arrange the fish strips in a single layer on the dehydrator trays.

To Dehydrate

1. Dehydrate at 165°F for 6 to 8 hours.

2. When dried, the fish jerky should be firm and tough and have a mild, fishy flavor. If it smells rancid, discard it, as this is a sign of spoilage.

continued on next page ▶

3. If your dehydrator doesn't get as hot as 165°F, use the highest temperature available to you. After the jerky is finished, place it on a paper-towel-lined baking sheet. Bake it in a preheated 275°F oven for 10 minutes to bring the internal temperature up to 165°F. Remove it from the oven. Use a paper towel to blot the surface of the jerky and remove any excess oil.

4. Cool the fish jerky to room temperature before you package it.

To Store

Fish jerky stored in a vacuum-sealed bag will last for 2 to 3 weeks at room temperature, 3 to 6 months in the refrigerator, or up to a year in the freezer.

SERVE IT UP: Take the fish jerky on road trips, camping, or other outdoor activities. It is lightweight and nutritious with concentrated energy to keep you energized. Fish jerky, like all jerky, is safe at room temperature for several days.

Shredded Chicken Breast

Prep and cook time: 30 minutes pressure cooker / 4½ hours slow cooker or stovetop
Dehydration time: 8 to 10 hours / **Yield:** 3 cups dehydrated chicken = 5 cups rehydrated

Chicken breast needs some extra preparation to make it suitable for dehydrating. You can dehydrate leftover chicken successfully, but it is difficult to rehydrate. Pressure-cooking chicken briefly in a pressure cooker solves this problem and creates a dehydrated chicken that is easy to rehydrate. However, for those who don't have a pressure cooker, a slow cooker or saucepan can be used instead. Boneless, skinless chicken breast is low in fat and is the best choice for dehydrated chicken.

2 pounds chicken breast, boneless, skinless

½ teaspoon sea salt

½ teaspoon freshly ground black pepper

¼ cup dried onions (page 75)

¼ cup dried parsley (page 95)

1 cup chicken stock

To Prepare

1. Pat the chicken breasts dry with a paper towel.

2. In a dish, combine the salt and pepper. Season the chicken breasts with the salt and pepper, covering both sides of each breast.

3. Add the onion, parsley, and chicken stock to the bottom of the insert for the pressure cooker, slow cooker, or saucepan. Place the chicken breasts into the stock and cover with a lid.

4. If using the pressure cooker, cook the chicken on high pressure for 6 minutes, following the manufacturer's directions for your pressure cooker. Let the pressure release naturally for 10 minutes, then use the safety directions that come with your pressure cooker to perform a quick release of the pressure. Remove the lid to the pressure cooker. Using tongs, remove the cooked chicken breasts. Let them sit for 10 minutes and cool so they can be handled safely.

continued on next page ▶

5. If using a slow cooker or the stovetop, simmer the chicken breasts in the herbed stock on medium heat for at least 4 hours to soften the proteins.

6. Using two forks, shred the chicken breasts into small strands.

7. Arrange the chicken into a single layer on the dehydrator trays.

To Dehydrate

1. Dehydrate at 145°F for 8 to 10 hours.

2. When dried, the chicken should be hard and brittle.

To Store

Dried chicken stored in vacuum-sealed bags will keep for up to a year in a cool, dark place.

ELEVATE YOUR DISH: The mild flavor of dehydrated chicken is the perfect base for spicier sauces such as marinara, curries, and creamy mushroom blends. Use these sauces to rehydrate the dehydrated chicken for a delicious alternative to chicken broth.

Shrimp

Prep time: 45 minutes / **Dehydration time:** 6 hours
Yield: 3 cups dehydrated shrimp = 4 cups rehydrated

Dried shrimp is versatile. Use it in casseroles, add it to a pasta sauce, or toss it into soup. This recipe starts with shelled, deveined shrimp that's ready to use immediately. There is no need to add salt, as the shrimp is naturally salty.

---

2 pounds frozen shrimp, cooked, peeled, and deveined

Juice and grated zest of 1 lemon

1 tablespoon olive oil

2 heads garlic

1 (1-inch) piece of ginger root

To Prepare

1. Thaw the shrimp in the refrigerator. It should still be slightly icy when you work with it.

2. Meanwhile, make the marinade. In a medium bowl, use a fork to lightly whisk the lemon juice and zest and the olive oil to combine.

3. Separate the cloves from each head of garlic. Peel each clove by crushing the clove with the flat part of a knife and removing the papery skin. Press the garlic cloves through a garlic press, one at a time. Add the crushed garlic to the lemon-olive oil mixture.

4. Peel the ginger with the edge of a spoon. Cut the ginger into fine cubes. Add the ginger to the lemon-olive oil mixture.

5. Place the shrimp in a colander. Rinse it with cold water, then drain it.

6. Cut each shrimp in half, crosswise. Then cut each half in half again, lengthwise through the vein channel on the back of the shrimp. (If there are any dark spots, scrape the dark vein out of the shrimp with the tip of your knife and discard the dark piece.)

continued on next page ▶

7. Add the prepared shrimp to the marinade. Stir it to coat all sides of the shrimp. Continue to add the shrimp as each one is cut. Stir the shrimp in the marinade after each addition, until all the shrimp have been added. Let the shrimp sit in the marinade for 10 more minutes, then drain it.

8. Arrange the shrimp in a single layer on the dehydrator trays.

To Dehydrate

1. Dehydrate at 145°F for 6 hours or until the shrimp is fully dried.

2. When dried, the shrimp should be hard and brittle with no moisture inside.

To Store

Dried shrimp stored in Mylar bags with oxygen absorbers will keep for up to a year at room temperature.

ELEVATE YOUR DISH: Spice up your flavors by adding cumin, turmeric, hot peppers, and other spices to the marinade before you add your prepared shrimp.

Tuna

Prep time: 10 minutes / **Dehydration time:** 3 to 4 hours
Yield: 2 cups dehydrated tuna = 3 cups rehydrated

This recipe has just one ingredient: Tuna packed in water. Use the dehydrated tuna for camping, hiking, and car trips, where managing a can may be awkward. My puppies do tricks for dehydrated tuna. Dried tuna is a healthy dog training treat that is economical to make at home. Tuna has a strong fishy fragrance though, so plan to dry tuna in a well-ventilated area, away from your living quarters, if possible.

3 (5-ounce) cans tuna, packed in water

To Prepare

1. Drain the cans of tuna. (If you have pets, reserve the tuna water for them!)

2. Line the dehydrator trays with fruit leather sheets.

3. Break up the tuna with a fork and spread it out on the lined dehydrator trays.

To Dehydrate

4. Dehydrate at 145°F for 3 to 4 hours.

5. When dried, the tuna pieces should be hard and dry.

To Store

Dried tuna stored in vacuum-sealed glass jars with oxygen absorbers will keep for 1 to 2 years.

ELEVATE YOUR DISH: Save time by dehydrating your tuna salad ingredients together. Add finely minced onions, celery, and sweet peppers to the tuna. Mix it together and spread it out in a single layer on the fruit-leather-sheet-lined dehydrator trays. Dry it as you would dehydrate canned tuna. When you are ready to make tuna salad, simply blend the dehydrated mixture with some mayonnaise. The tuna salad will be ready to spread on your bread in a few minutes.

Chili Mac · 138

PART III

Dehydrated Snacks & Meals

Dehydrated snacks and meals can save you money and help you reach your health goals. Replace unhealthy processed snacks with dehydrated chips, crackers, and energy bars made from healthy veggies, fruit, seeds, and nuts. Fruit and vegetable leathers make delicious, chewy snacks for lunch bags and road trips.

Dehydrated meals aren't just for hikers; they can also make weeknight meal planning quick and easy. With dehydrated meals in your pantry, you can skip the takeout and enjoy home-cooked meals literally in the time it takes to boil water.

In this section, you'll find recipes for snacks that are better than store-bought. Don't settle for heavily processed snacks when you can make your own, control the ingredients, and add the toppings or spices that you like best.

You'll also find easy recipes to make from dehydrated ingredients so your pantry food becomes an integral part of your everyday cooking. You'll find soup, stew, and casserole recipes that are perfect for those busy days when you only have time to throw a few ingredients together.

CHAPTER 7

Snacks

Dehydrated snacks are nutrient-dense as well as being low in sugar and fat. Making your own dehydrated snacks at home will save you money and allow you to control the ingredients.

Fruit leather is a good way to use small amounts of fruit that become soft, bruised, or overripe and are unsuitable for dehydrating alone. Fruit leather is made from fruit or vegetable purees. The purees will seep through the holes on a regular dehydrator tray, so make sure to line the trays with fruit leather sheets made for your dehydrator (or use parchment paper or plastic wrap). The outside of the tray will dry first, so to avoid brittle edges, make the perimeter a little thicker than the center as you spread the puree to allow for even drying.

Once the fruit leather appears done and is dry and leathery on the surface, there may still be some areas in the center of the sheet that are underdone. Peel the fruit leather off the sheet and flip it to dry the other side. You'll want to package fruit leather while it is still warm.

Crackers and energy bars also benefit from tray liners. The dense dough should be spread thinly over the tray liner, to speed drying time. These foods can be made even healthier by drying at lower temperatures to retain nutrients and enzymes.

Root vegetables such as beets, parsnips, and sweet potatoes make delicious, crunchy chips for snacking and are a healthy alternative to potato chips. Slicing these veggies thinly using a mandoline will speed up prep time and ensure even slices, which translates to even drying.

Other vegetables also make crunchy chip-like snacks. You'll find a recipe for kale chips in this chapter, but you can use this technique for any leafy greens. Zucchini and cucumber make mild-flavored chips that can be dressed up with herbs and spices. Chips will lose their crunch in storage but can be renewed by placing them back in the dehydrator for a few minutes.

Energy bars use dehydrated fruit and nuts, giving you a wide variety of flavors and combinations to satisfy your hunger on the go. Dehydrate the dough at low temperatures to maintain their nutrients and enzymes.

Apple Fruit Leather

Prep and cook time: 30 minutes / **Dehydration time:** 9 hours / **Yield:** 6 servings

The first step in making any fruit leather is to make applesauce. Canned applesauce can be substituted for the apples in this recipe. Softer apples, such as Macintosh, Gala, and Golden Delicious, are the best for fruit leather.

**6 medium apples, or
2 cups prepared
applesauce**

¼ cup water

**1 tablespoon sugar
(optional)**

ELEVATE YOUR DISH:
Vary the fruit leather flavors by substituting half the applesauce with another fruit, such as strawberries, pears, or peaches.

1. Wash the apples in a sink of cold water. Peel and core the apples and cut them into quarters.

2. In a saucepan over medium heat, cook the apple pieces in the water. Simmer until the apples soften and can be easily mashed with a fork, about 10 minutes. Stir the apples occasionally to prevent them from sticking. Cool them to room temperature.

3. In a blender or food processor, process the apples for 1 minute on medium speed, until the applesauce is smooth. Add the sugar to taste, if using.

4. Pour the applesauce on a dehydrator tray lined with a fruit leather sheet. Using a spatula, spread the applesauce across the tray, making the perimeter slightly thicker than the center.

5. Dehydrate at 140°F for 8 hours. When the fruit leather is dry to the touch, peel it off the fruit leather sheet and flip it. Continue drying the fruit leather for 1 hour, or until there are no moist spots left on the fruit leather.

To Store

Cut the fruit leather into 6 even pieces. Cut parchment paper the same size as the fruit leather pieces. Lay the fruit leather on top of the parchment paper. Beginning at the narrow end, tightly roll the fruit leather and the parchment paper. Place the wrapped fruit leather in a freezer bag or airtight container for storage. Fruit leather will keep for up to 6 months at room temperature.

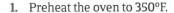

NUT-FREE · GLUTEN-FREE · VEGAN

Beet Chips

Prep and cook time: 1 hour, 20 minutes / **Dehydration time:** 6 hours / **Yield:** 4 cups beet chips

Beet chips are a healthy alternative to potato chips, as they are crunchy, sweet, and fat-free. Bake the beets first to intensify their sweetness.

6 large beets

2 cups water

¼ teaspoon sea salt

ELEVATE YOUR DISH:
Season your beet chips with spices that meld well with the sweet, earthy flavor of the beets, such as garlic powder, dill, or ranch dressing powder. Sprinkle the spices on the beet slices before you dehydrate them.

1. Preheat the oven to 350°F.

2. Using a vegetable brush, scrub the beets under cold water. Trim off any leaves without cutting into the beet. Trim the root close to the main part of the beet.

3. Place the whole beets in a roasting pan. Add the water to the bottom of the pan to prevent the beets from sticking. Bake for 1 hour, or until the beets are soft when pierced with a fork. Remove from the oven and transfer the beets to a large bowl of cold water to cool them quickly.

4. When the beets are cool enough to handle, remove their skins underwater by slipping them off with your fingers. Cut off the rougher top of the beet.

5. Using a mandoline, slice the beets into ⅛-inch slices. Place the sliced beets in a single layer on the dehydrator trays. Lightly sprinkle the beet slices with the sea salt.

6. Dehydrate at 145°F for 6 hours, or until the beets are dry and crisp.

7. While the beet chips are still warm, lift them off the dehydrator trays by gently flexing the trays. The edges of the beets will lift, making them easy to peel off the trays. Place the beet chips in a shallow dish to cool. The beet chips will crisp up as they cool.

To Store
The beet chips will stay crisp for up to 3 months in zip-top bags, at room temperature.

Candied Ginger

Prep and cook time: 1 hour / **Dehydration time:** 4 hours / **Yield:** 1 cup

Candied ginger is warm and spicy, with a chewy texture. The pectin from the lemons gives this spicy treat its chewy texture.

1 large piece ginger root, peeled and cut into ⅛-inch-thick slices

Juice and grated zest of 2 medium lemons

3½ cups water

3 cups sugar, divided

½ teaspoon butter

MIX IT UP: Cut candied ginger into fine strips and use it as a topping for ice cream, cream cheese, cream soups, salads, or noodle dishes. It adds warmth and sweetness to sweet—and savory—foods.

1. In a saucepan, combine the ginger slices and lemon juice and zest. Add the water, and simmer for 30 minutes, until the ginger is soft. Add 2½ cups of the sugar, stirring until all the sugar is dissolved.

2. Simmer over medium heat until the mixture comes to a rapid boil. Stir in the butter, which will reduce the foaming. Stir occasionally to keep the ginger from sticking to the bottom of the pot. When the mixture reaches 220°F on a candy thermometer, remove the pot from the heat. (To test the temperature without a candy thermometer, drop a tiny amount in a bowl of cold water. When it is ready it will form a thin thread.)

3. Line a baking sheet with parchment paper. Using a slotted spoon, remove the ginger slices from the sugar mixture and place them in a single layer on a cooling rack placed over the prepared baking sheet. Reserve the ginger syrup for another use.

4. Put the remaining ½ cup of sugar into a bowl. Using tongs, dredge each slice of ginger in sugar, coating both sides.

5. Arrange the candied ginger in a single layer on the dehydrator trays. Dehydrate at 130°F for 4 hours, or until they are firm and dry.

To Store

Candied ginger stored in a vacuum-sealed glass jar will keep for up to 5 years.

Corn Chips

Prep time: 10 minutes / **Dehydration time:** 8 hours / **Yield:** 30 chips

These dehydrator corn chips are ideal for cheesy nachos. Sweet and salty, they are made with dehydrated sweet corn and flaxseed. You can make them plain or get creative and add spices to the batter before you spread them out on the tray. The prep time is fast for these when you already have the dehydrated sweet corn in your pantry!

2 cups dried corn (page 68)

¼ cup flaxseed

3 dried lime slices (optional) (page 39)

½ teaspoon sea salt

1 cup warm water

1. In a blender or food processor, combine the corn, flaxseed, lime slices (if using), salt, and water. Pulse on medium speed until the mixture is blended and resembles coarse dough. If the mixture is too dry to spread easily, add more water, 1 tablespoon at a time, until it can easily be spread on the dehydrator sheets.

2. Line the dehydrator trays with fruit leather sheets. Using a spatula, spread the mixture on the lined dehydrator trays in an even ⅛-inch-thick layer.

3. Dehydrate at 150°F for 8 hours. After 4 hours, cut the chips with a knife into 2-inch triangles, without cutting through the fruit leather sheets, and continue to dry for 4 hours. The corn chips are done when they are hard and crispy. The edges will curl up slightly when they are done.

To Store

Dried corn chips stored in Mylar bags with oxygen absorbers will keep for up to 6 months. You can always crisp them up again by dehydrating for 1 hour at 155°F.

ELEVATE YOUR DISH: Make spicy corn chips by adding a light sprinkling of chili powder, chipotle pepper spice (page 85), garlic powder, or a few drops of hot sauce to the batter before you spread it on the lined dehydrator trays. The spice will permeate the chips for a spicy snack that goes well with guacamole.

Fruit & Nut Energy Bars

Prep time: 1 hour, 15 minutes / **Dehydration time:** 20 hours / **Yield:** 24 bars

Pack these sweet and crunchy bars for hikes or car trips to give you energy, fast! These are a must on our family ski trips and snowshoeing adventures. To preserve the probiotics in the yogurt, these bars are dehydrated at a low temperature.

1 cup dried fruit, such as apples, peaches, or pears

1½ cups yogurt, plain or flavored

2 cups dried dates (page 42)

¼ cup ground flaxseed

¼ cup chia seeds

½ cup sesame seeds

½ cup slivered almonds

¼ cup cashews

1. In a small bowl, mix together the dried fruit and yogurt until combined. Let it sit for 1 hour to soften the fruit.

2. To the bowl of a food processor, pour in the yogurt mixture, dates, flaxseed, and chia seeds. Process on medium speed for 1 to 2 minutes, until a chunky paste forms. Transfer the mixture to a bowl.

3. Stir in the sesame seeds, almonds, and cashews until the mixture is well blended.

4. Divide the batter in half. Spread each half on a fruit leather sheet or parchment-paper-lined dehydrator tray to make a sheet of dough ¼ inch thick.

5. Dehydrate at 105°F for 20 hours. After 15 hours, when the top of the bar is firm and dry, peel the bars off the fruit leather sheets. Flip the bars and put them back in the dehydrator for 5 hours or until they are dry and firm.

6. Cut them into 2-by-4-inch bars.

To Store

Stored in an airtight container, the bars will keep for up to 3 months. They will keep for up to a year in the freezer.

ELEVATE YOUR DISH: Add 2 tablespoons finely chopped candied ginger (page 126), or ¼ teaspoon smoky chipotle pepper powder (page 85) to the bars when you add the nuts for a warming snack for wintery days.

Kale Chips

Prep time: 20 minutes / **Dehydration time:** 5 hours / **Yield:** 4 cups

---

Crunchy, zesty kale chips earn their place on the crudité tray by adding color and texture. My favorite kale for this recipe is the Lacinato ("dinosaur") kale variety. The texture of the leaves holds on to the dressing well, making the finished kale chips more flavorful.

---

8 cups kale, washed

2 tablespoons extra-virgin olive oil

Juice and grated zest of 1 lemon

1 garlic clove, peeled and minced

¼ teaspoon sea salt

1. Remove the center rib from the kale leaves. Tear the kale leaves into 1½- to 2-inch pieces. Place the leaves in a large bowl and set aside.

2. In a small bowl, whisk together the olive oil, lemon juice and zest, garlic, and sea salt until it lightens in color. Pour this dressing over the kale.

3. Using clean hands, massage the dressing into the kale leaves until the leaves darken and the dressing is uniformly dispersed throughout the kale.

4. Spread the kale in a single layer over 4 dehydrator trays.

5. Dehydrate at 135°F for 5 hours. When dried, the kale should be crisp and brittle.

To Store

Kale Chips will keep for 4 weeks when stored in an airtight container in a cool, dry place. Due to the added oil, they have a shorter shelf life.

PREP LIKE A PRO: Stem several kale leaves at one time. On a cutting board, stack the washed kale leaves in a pile with the largest leaves on the bottom and the center stem lined up through the layers. Cut on either side of the stem, cutting through all layers. Break the leaves into bite-size pieces by tearing a stack of 3 or 4 leaves at the same time.

Lemon-Ginger-Turmeric Drink

Prep time: 10 minutes / **Yield:** 16 (8-ounce) servings

Make this energizing, detoxifying drink mix using dried lemon slices (page 39), dried ginger (page 88), and dried turmeric (page 88) from your dried food pantry.

3 cups dried lemon slices

1 cup dried turmeric slices

1 cup dried ginger slices

½ teaspoon freshly ground black pepper

1. In a blender, blend the lemon slices on high speed to powder them. Transfer the powder to a small bowl.

2. Combine the turmeric and ginger in the blender. Blend on high speed to powder them. Add them to the bowl with the powdered lemon. Add the pepper to the bowl.

3. Whisk this mixture together until it is uniformly blended. Transfer the mixture to an airtight jar.

To Store

The drink mixture will keep in a tightly sealed jar, at room temperature, for up to 6 months.

REHYDRATION INSTRUCTIONS: Add 1 tablespoon of the lemon drink to an 8-ounce mug of hot or cold water. Stir well to blend it. Sweeten with honey to taste, if desired.

SERVE IT UP: Make golden milk using this drink mixture by adding 1 tablespoon of the drink mix to 8 ounces heated coconut milk or almond milk. Stir the heated milk with a whisk to foam it before stirring in the drink mix.

Pumpkin Spice Latte Leather

Prep and cook time: 20 minutes / **Dehydration time:** 20 hours / **Yield:** 6 pieces

Use vegetables and fruit together in fruit leather recipes. When used alone, vegetables lack the pectin needed to give the fruit leather the needed chewy texture. But when pectin-rich fruit like apples are added, even vegetables can create dessert-worthy treats. Make this pumpkin spice fruit leather in the fall when squash and pumpkins are in season.

6 apples, peeled and cored

¼ cup coconut milk

1 cup cooked pumpkin or winter squash

1 tablespoon honey

½ teaspoon powdered ginger

1 teaspoon cinnamon

½ teaspoon freshly grated nutmeg

PREP LIKE A PRO: Use 1 cup canned pumpkin and 2 cups canned applesauce for this recipe and skip the extra preparation steps. If using canned goods, begin preparation at step 2.

1. In a saucepan over medium heat, combine the apples and coconut milk. Cook until the apples are soft, about 10 minutes.

2. Transfer the apples to a blender jar and add the pumpkin, honey, ginger, cinnamon, and nutmeg. Cover and blend on high for 1 to 1½ minutes, until smooth and well blended.

3. Transfer the mixture to a fruit-leather-sheet-lined dehydrator tray. Using a spatula, spread the mixture ¼ inch thick across the sheet.

4. Dehydrate at 145°F for 20 hours. After 15 hours, peel the pumpkin leather off the fruit leather sheets, then flip it and continue drying for 5 hours until it is dry and pliable.

5. While still warm, cut the pumpkin leather into 2- by 12-inch strips. Place each strip on a piece of parchment paper cut to the same size. Roll the fruit leather with the parchment paper into a tight roll. Secure with a piece of tape.

To Store

Pumpkin Spice Latte Leather will keep for up to 1 year when stored in an airtight container in a cool, dry place protected from heat and light.

Seed Crackers

Prep time: 15 minutes / **Dehydration time:** 10 hours / **Yield:** 36 crackers

I make a double batch of these seed crackers every week. They are full of crunch, fiber, and flavor. Held together with flaxseed and chia seeds, they are at home on a cheese board, or beside a bowl of hearty soup.

½ **cup ground flaxseed**

½ **cup chia seeds**

½ **cup hot water**

2 **tablespoons olive oil**

½ **cup pumpkin seeds**

1 **cup almond flour**

½ **cup sesame seeds**

½ **teaspoon sea salt**

1. In a small bowl, combine the flaxseed, chia seeds, and water. While the mixture is still warm, stir in the olive oil. Set it aside to cool.

2. In a large bowl, combine the pumpkin seeds, almond flour, sesame seeds, and sea salt.

3. Pour the flax mixture into the seed blend and mix to form a stiff, pliable dough. If the dough is too stiff, add more water, 1 tablespoon at a time, until the dough is firm, but can be rolled easily.

4. Divide the dough in half. Roll each half of the dough between two fruit leather sheets until it is ⅛ inch thick. Remove the top fruit leather sheet. Place the bottom fruit leather sheet with the dough on a dehydrator tray. Repeat this process with the remaining dough.

5. Using a pizza cutter, and being careful not to pierce the fruit leather sheets, slice each half of the cracker dough into 2-inch crackers.

6. Dehydrate at 145°F for 10 hours. After 8 hours, peel the fruit leather sheets off the crackers, flip the crackers, and dehydrate the other side for 2 more hours.

7. When fully dried, break the crackers apart along the cut lines.

To Store

Seed Crackers will keep for up to 4 weeks when stored in an airtight container at room temperature. For long-term storage, store the crackers in the freezer for up to 6 months.

Zucchini or Cucumber Chips

Prep time: 15 minutes / **Dehydration time:** 10 hours / **Yield:** 2 cups

Use the abundant summer supply of cucumbers and zucchini to make these healthy and savory chips. For the best results, use small zucchini and cucumbers that are no more than 1½ inches in diameter and have very little seed development. Hothouse English cucumbers can also be used for this recipe.

4 small zucchini or cucumbers (or one long English cucumber)

½ teaspoon garlic powder (page 87)

½ teaspoon onion powder (page 75)

½ teaspoon dried dill seed (page 84)

½ teaspoon dried chives

¼ teaspoon sea salt

¼ teaspoon freshly ground black pepper

1. Wash the zucchini or cucumber. Cut off both ends and discard.

2. Using a mandoline, slice the zucchini or cucumber into ⅛-inch slices.

3. Arrange the pieces in a single layer on a dehydrator tray.

4. In a small bowl, combine the garlic powder, onion powder, dill seed, chives, salt, and pepper. Sprinkle the herb mixture over the sliced vegetables on their exposed side.

5. Dehydrate at 145°F for 10 hours. After 7 hours, flip the slices, and continue dehydrating for 3 hours until the slices are crisp and brittle.

To Store

Zucchini or Cucumber Chips will keep for 3 to 4 months when stored in an airtight container at room temperature. You can crisp them up again by dehydrating for 1 hour at 145°F.

PREP LIKE A PRO: Commercial spice mixes can be used in place of the herbs, salt, and pepper in this recipe. Use dry salad dressing mixes such as ranch dressing, Italian, or garden dill to elevate this dish and save you time.

CHAPTER 8

Meals & Sides

W hether you need a quick weeknight dinner, you're planning for a camping trip, or you're traveling, dehydrated ingredients can offer nutritious and delicious meals to meet your needs. In this chapter, you'll find two types of meals: main courses that highlight dehydrated ingredients you have in your pantry, and family favorites that you make in bulk and dehydrate for future meals.

When dehydrated ingredients are the star of the meal, most of the prep work has already been done. Soups, stews, and casseroles can be assembled quickly, reducing cleanup time, too.

When making a soup or stew using dehydrated ingredients, ingredients may be rehydrated directly in the broth, making an almost-instant soup or stew. When you need a lunch on the go, add dehydrated soup mix to an insulated mug. Top it off with boiling water, and it will be steaming hot and ready to enjoy at lunchtime.

When making a casserole from dehydrated ingredients, rehydrate each ingredient individually and assemble the casserole using the rehydrated ingredients. This makes an attractive presentation and gives the food a familiar appearance to alleviate the fears of discerning eaters.

When dehydrating complete meals that include cooked meat, fish, or poultry, dehydrate at 145°F or higher to minimize the chance of bacterial contamination. Spread the food in a single layer in the dehydrator to speed up dehydrating times. Because these meals contain ingredients with various densities, parts of the meal may dehydrate faster than other parts. Stir the food periodically while it is drying to ensure even, fast drying.

If your dehydrator has trays with large holes, use tray liners or fruit leather sheets to prevent dried food from falling through the holes as it shrinks. Package fully dried meals in glass jars or Mylar bags with oxygen absorbers to preserve flavor, aroma, and texture. Consult the recipes for specific instructions for preparation, dehydrating, and rehydrating.

Black Bean Chili

Prep time: 10 minutes / **Cook time:** 40 minutes / **Dehydration time:** 12 hours / **Serves:** 4

Chili is a hearty comfort meal that is quick to prepare from canned beans. This meal uses the chipotle peppers, celery, onions, and the sweet peppers recipe found in chapter 4. If you choose to use fresh ingredients in place of dried, double the amounts called for in the recipe.

2 (15-ounce) cans black beans

1 (28-ounce) can tomatoes, stewed

1 teaspoon chili powder

½ teaspoon cumin

2 garlic cloves, minced

1 to 3 chipotle peppers, crushed (page 85)

¼ cup dried celery (page 67)

¼ cup dried onions (page 75)

¼ cup dried sweet peppers (page 76)

½ teaspoon salt

1. Drain the beans and rinse them well. Pour them into a stockpot and add the tomatoes, chili powder, cumin, garlic, chipotle peppers, celery, onions, sweet peppers, and salt. Stir well to combine.

2. Cook the chili over medium heat until it comes to a boil. Lower the heat and simmer for 30 minutes. Remove the chili from the heat, and stir it to blend the ingredients.

3. Serve immediately, or dehydrate for future meals. To dehydrate, cool the chili to just warm. Line the dehydrator trays with fruit leather sheets. Spoon the chili onto the lined trays and spread it into a thin layer. Dehydrate at 145°F for 12 hours until the beans are hard and brittle.

To Store

Dried Black Bean Chili stored in sealed Mylar bags with oxygen absorbers and kept in a cool, dry place will keep for up to 5 years.

To Rehydrate

In a medium saucepan, combine 1 cup of the chili and 1½ cups boiling water. Cover and reconstitute for 40 minutes. Stir. Heat the chili over low heat until the beans are softened, about 20 minutes.

SERVE IT UP: Serve the chili with salsa, guacamole, fresh cilantro, lime juice, shredded cheese, and corn chips (to make your own, see page 127).

Butternut Squash Soup

Prep time: 10 minutes / **Cook time:** 45 minutes / **Serves:** 4

This simple soup is pure comfort food. Rich in warming spices, it is a hearty winter meal. Serve it with Seed Crackers (page 132) or crusty bread.

1 butternut squash, peeled and seeded

2 cups vegetable stock

3 cups water, divided

¼ cup dried onions (page 75)

¼ cup dried sweet peppers (page 76)

¼ cup dried celery (page 67)

1 teaspoon cumin

1 teaspoon dried turmeric (page 88)

1 teaspoon dried ginger (page 88)

3 garlic cloves, peeled and minced

1 cup coconut cream (for serving)

1. Slice and cube the butternut squash into ½-inch cubes. Place the cubed squash in a medium saucepan with the vegetable stock and 2 cups of water. Cover and simmer over medium heat for 20 minutes, until the butternut squash is soft.

2. Meanwhile, in a small bowl, combine the onions, sweet peppers, and celery. Cover the dried vegetables with 1 cup of warm water and let them sit for 30 minutes to rehydrate them.

3. Stir the rehydrated vegetables into the cooked butternut squash. Add the cumin, turmeric, ginger, and garlic to the squash mixture. Cover and simmer over medium heat for 15 minutes. Turn off the heat.

4. Using an immersion blender, process the butternut soup until it is smooth. Alternatively, the soup may be cooled to just warm, pureed in a blender on medium speed, then reheated before serving.

5. Pour the coconut cream into the blended soup and stir to combine. Serve immediately.

PREP LIKE A PRO: Save time by making this recipe with dried winter squash (page 81). Rehydrate the squash in the vegetable broth for 30 minutes before proceeding with the recipe.

Chili Mac

Prep time: 10 minutes / **Cook time:** 30 minutes / **Dehydration time:** 15 hours / **Serves:** 4

Chili Mac is a fast weeknight meal made with chili and cooked macaroni. My family likes it topped with cheddar cheese and a dollop of sour cream for a creamy finish.

4 cups macaroni or shells

1 (28-ounce) can diced tomatoes

1 medium onion, diced

1 green pepper, seeded and diced

2 garlic cloves, peeled and minced

1 teaspoon dried hot peppers (page 76)

1 teaspoon chili powder

½ teaspoon sea salt

1 (15-ounce) can kidney beans

¼ cup cilantro, finely chopped

1. Cook the macaroni according to the package directions, but for a few minutes less so the pasta is al dente. Rinse it in a colander under cold water. Drain the macaroni and set it aside.

2. Meanwhile, in a medium saucepan, add the tomatoes and their juices. Stir in the onion, green pepper, garlic, hot pepper, chili powder, and salt. Simmer over medium heat until the mixture begins to steam, about 5 minutes.

3. Drain the beans and rinse under cold water, until the rinsing water stops foaming. Add the beans to the tomato mixture. Simmer over medium heat for 20 minutes until the mixture begins to thicken. Remove from the heat and stir in the cilantro.

4. Add the macaroni to the saucepan. Stir gently to coat the macaroni with the tomato mixture.

5. Line the dehydrator trays with fruit leather sheets. Spread the Chili Mac evenly over the lined dehydrator trays in a thin layer. Dehydrate at 145°F for 15 hours or until the mixture is dry and brittle and the beans crush easily when pressed.

To Store

Dried Chili Mac stored in Mylar bags with oxygen absorbers and stored in a cool, dry place will keep for up to 5 years.

To Rehydrate

In a medium saucepan, combine 1 cup of the Chili Mac and 1½ cups boiling water. Simmer, covered, over low heat for 10 minutes. Remove from the heat and reconstitute for 15 more minutes with the lid on.

SERVE IT UP: Top the mac with cheddar cheese and ¼ cup breadcrumbs. Bake it under a broiler just long enough to melt the cheese and serve hot.

Coconut Shrimp & Rice Curry

Prep time: 20 minutes / **Cook time:** 45 minutes / **Dehydration time:** 12 hours / **Serves:** 4

Packed with aromatic spices, this curry is so flavorful, it's like having restaurant-quality food at home!

1 cup basmati rice

2 (14-ounce) cans low-fat coconut milk, divided

½ cup water

1 pound large cooked shrimp, shelled and deveined

1 (28-ounce) can diced tomatoes

¼ cup tapioca starch

1 teaspoon onion powder

½ teaspoon garlic powder

1 teaspoon garam masala

½ teaspoon powdered ginger

1 teaspoon dried hot peppers (page 76)

Juice and grated zest of 1 lime

¼ cup fresh cilantro, finely chopped, for garnish (optional)

1. In a saucepan over medium heat, cook the rice, 1 can of coconut milk, and the water, until the rice is tender, about 30 minutes. Remove from the heat and set aside.

2. Rinse the shrimp under cold water. Drain.

3. To the saucepan, add the remaining can of coconut milk and the tomatoes. Whisk in the tapioca starch (to prevent lumps). Add the onion powder, garlic powder, garam masala, ginger, hot pepper, and lime juice and zest. Simmer over medium heat until the mixture thickens, stirring occasionally to prevent scorching. Add the shrimp and cook for 5 more minutes. Remove from the heat.

4. Mix the coconut shrimp mixture and the coconut rice, blending only enough to coat the rice. Serve immediately with fresh cilantro or dehydrate the dish for later. To dehydrate, spread the coconut shrimp and rice in a thin, even layer on the dehydrator trays lined with fruit leather sheets. Dehydrate at 145°F for 12 hours or until the coconut shrimp mixture is hard and brittle.

To Store

Dried Coconut Shrimp & Rice Curry stored in Mylar bags with oxygen absorbers and stored in a cool, dry place will keep for up to 5 years.

To Rehydrate

In a medium saucepan, combine 1 cup of the shrimp and rice mixture and 1½ cups boiling water. Simmer, covered, over low heat for 10 minutes. Remove from the heat and reconstitute for 15 more minutes with the lid on.

Curry Chicken with Rice

Prep time: 20 minutes / **Cook time:** 30 minutes / **Dehydration time:** 14 hours / **Serves:** 8

This is a favorite weekend meal in my home. Starting with dehydrated ingredients saves preparation time, so feel free to substitute 2 cups of dehydrated chicken breast (page 115) in place of the chicken breasts called for in the recipe.

2 pounds boneless, skinless chicken breasts

11 cups water, divided

5 garlic cloves, minced

1 teaspoon garam masala

1 teaspoon cumin

1 teaspoon turmeric

1 teaspoon dried hot peppers (page 76)

¼ cup dried onions (page 75)

¼ cup dried sweet peppers (page 76)

1 (14-ounce) can low-fat coconut milk

½ teaspoon sea salt

4 cups basmati rice

1. Slice the chicken breasts into ½-inch cubes. In a skillet over medium heat, heat the chicken and about ½ cup water, stirring to sear all sides. Add more water if needed, to prevent the chicken from sticking.

2. Stir the garlic, garam masala, cumin, turmeric, and 2 cups more water into the chicken. Add the hot peppers, onion, sweet peppers, coconut milk, and salt to the mixture and stir.

3. Simmer the curried chicken, uncovered, until the liquid is reduced by half and the skillet is bubbling and fragrant, about 20 minutes. Stir occasionally to prevent the sauce from sticking. When the sauce is thickened, remove the skillet from the heat.

4. Meanwhile, place the rice in a large saucepan with 8 cups of water. Cover the saucepan and cook the rice over medium-low heat for 20 minutes, until all the water is absorbed and the rice is tender. Set aside.

5. The chicken can be served over the rice, as a meal, or both can be dehydrated. Dehydrate the curried chicken and rice separately and store separately. Cool the rice and the curry chicken. Line the dehydrator trays with fruit leather sheets or parchment paper. Spread the rice in a thin layer on two dehydrator sheets. Spread the curry chicken on 2 dehydrator sheets. Dehydrate at 145°F for 14 hours. The rice is done when it is hard and brittle. The chicken will be dry and leathery when finished.

To Store

Package the rice and chicken separately in vacuum-sealed glass jars or in Mylar bags with oxygen absorbers. If kept in a cool, dry place, the rice and the curry chicken will keep for up to 5 years.

To Rehydrate

To rehydrate the rice, in a medium saucepan, combine 1 cup of the rice with 1 cup boiling water. Cover and reconstitute for 15 minutes. To rehydrate the chicken, in a medium saucepan, combine 1 cup of the chicken mixture and 1½ cups boiling water or chicken stock. Simmer, covered, over low heat for 15 minutes. Remove from the heat and reconstitute for 15 more minutes.

ELEVATE YOUR DISH: Add 1 (28-ounce) can diced tomatoes or 1 cup dried tomatoes (page 80) to the sauce when you add the coconut milk to the pan, and you will transform this dish into butter chicken, one of my family's favorite curry dishes.

Spicy Tomato Rice

Prep time: 10 minutes / **Cook time:** 45 minutes / **Dehydration time:** 8 hours / **Serves:** 2

Make this spicy tomato rice in a large batch and dehydrate for several meals. The dish cooks up quickly and dehydrates overnight.

1 (28-ounce) can diced tomatoes

1 teaspoon dried chipotle pepper (page 76)

½ onion, finely diced

1 green pepper, finely diced

1 celery stalk, finely diced

2 garlic cloves, minced

1 cup short-grain white rice

1 teaspoon paprika (page 94)

1. In a large saucepan, combine the tomatoes, chipotle pepper, onion, green pepper, celery, and garlic. Simmer over medium heat until the vegetables are softened and translucent, about 20 minutes.

2. Stir in the white rice. Continue cooking until the mixture begins to bubble. Reduce the heat to low. Cover the saucepan and simmer until the rice is soft and the tomato liquid has been absorbed, about 30 minutes. Stir occasionally to prevent scorching. Remove the rice and tomato mixture from the heat. Stir in the paprika.

3. Fluff the spicy tomato rice with a fork to separate the grains.

4. Serve immediately, or dehydrate: Spread the cooled tomato rice onto dehydrator trays lined with fruit leather sheets. Dehydrate at 145°F for 8 hours, or until the rice is hard and brittle.

To Store

Dried Spicy Tomato Rice stored in Mylar bags with oxygen absorbers will keep for up to 5 years.

To Rehydrate

In a medium saucepan, combine 1 cup of Spicy Tomato Rice and 1 cup boiling water. Cover the saucepan and reconstitute for 25 minutes.

SERVE IT UP: This can be dressed up by adding extra protein, such as grated cheese, shrimp, or chicken. Served with a salad or vegetable side it becomes a complete meal!

Vegetable Soup Blend

Prep time: 10 minutes / **Rehydrating Time:** 30 minutes / **Serves:** 8

I keep this on hand for quick weeknight dinners or spontaneous trips. Use your dehydrated vegetables for this soup blend. This soup blend also makes a lovely gift for a neighbor or friend. Don't forget to add a recipe with your gift!

1 cup dried diced potatoes (page 77)

1 cup dried diced carrots (page 66)

½ cup dried diced celery (page 67)

½ cup dried tomatoes (page 80)

½ cup dried spinach (page 71)

¼ cup dried diced onions (page 75)

¼ cup dried diced sweet peppers (page 76)

¼ cup dried parsley (page 95)

Salt

Freshly ground black pepper

1. In a large bowl, combine the potatoes, carrots, celery, tomatoes, spinach, onions, sweet peppers, and parsley. Mix with a spoon until it is uniformly blended.

2. Transfer the blend to a glass jar.

To Store

Dried Vegetable Soup Blend stored in a vacuum-sealed glass jar and protected from light and heat will keep for up to 5 years.

To Rehydrate

In a medium saucepan, combine 1 cup of Vegetable Soup Blend with 4 cups boiling water or broth. Simmer over low heat until the vegetables soften, about 30 minutes. Add salt and pepper to taste.

SERVE IT UP: Make a hot lunch in a hurry. In the morning, add ½ cup of this dry soup mix plus a liberal sprinkle of salt and pepper to a 16-ounce insulated vacuum-flask container. Fill the container with boiling water. Cap tightly. Open the vacuum flask at noon, stir the contents, and your healthy hot lunch is ready to eat.

Fajita Chicken

Prep time: 15 minutes / **Cook time:** 40 minutes / **Dehydration time:** 12 hours / **Serves:** 4

Fajita chicken can be served over rice or tortillas. Start with leftover chicken and flavor it with sweet peppers, onions, tomatoes, and smoky chipotle peppers for a mouthwatering midweek meal.

1½ pounds boneless, skinless chicken breasts

2 tablespoons olive oil

1½ cups chicken broth

¼ cup dried sweet red and green peppers (page 76)

¼ cup dried onions (page 75)

2 garlic cloves, peeled and crushed

1 teaspoon chili powder

1 teaspoon dried chipotle peppers, crushed (page 76)

½ cup dried tomatoes (page 80)

1. Cut the chicken into ½-inch strips. In a skillet over medium heat, heat the oil. Sear the chicken on all sides.

2. Add the broth, peppers, onions, garlic, chili powder, chipotle peppers, and tomatoes. Simmer over medium heat, stirring occasionally, until the dehydrated vegetables are soft and the stock is reduced by half, about 30 minutes.

3. Serve immediately with rice or tortillas or dehydrate for later. To dehydrate, spread the fajita chicken in a thin, even layer over dehydrator trays lined with fruit leather sheets. Dehydrate at 145°F for 12 hours until the fajita chicken is hard and brittle.

To Store

Dried Fajita Chicken stored in Mylar bags with an oxygen absorber and kept in a cool, dry place will keep for up to 5 years.

To Rehydrate

In a medium saucepan, combine 1 cup of Fajita Chicken and 1½ cups boiling water. Simmer, covered, over low heat for 10 minutes. Remove from the heat and reconstitute for 15 minutes, with the lid on.

PREP LIKE A PRO: When you dry the peppers, cut some ½ inch wide before dehydrating. Use these peppers for stir-fries and Fajita Chicken, and for other dishes in which they play a leading role.

Ginger Beef & Broccoli Bowl

Prep time: 15 minutes / **Cook time:** 30 minutes / **Dehydration time:** 12 hours / **Serves:** 4

Healthier than takeout, with less fat, this dish offers a gingery warmth that pairs well with rice or noodles.

1 pound sirloin steak, fat trimmed, cut into ¼-inch pieces

2 tablespoons tapioca starch, divided

2 cups cold water, divided

1 tablespoon grated ginger

1 bunch scallions (green and white parts), sliced

2 garlic cloves, minced

2 tablespoons tamari

¼ cup beef broth

4 cups broccoli florets

1. In a medium bowl, dredge the steak slices in 1 tablespoon of tapioca starch, covering all sides. Set aside.

2. In a large saucepan, add 1¾ cups of the water. Simmer over medium heat till the pan is hot and the water starts bubbling. Stir in the ginger, scallions, garlic, tamari, and beef broth. Simmer gently until the scallions are limp, about 2 minutes. Add the steak and simmer for 5 more minutes, stirring occasionally until the steak is brown.

3. In a small bowl, pour in the remaining ¼ cup of water and add the remaining tablespoon of tapioca starch. Stir with a fork to remove any lumps. Add this mixture to the saucepan, stirring to prevent lumps. Add the broccoli florets, and continue stirring for 2 minutes until the broccoli turns bright green and the sauce thickens.

4. Serve immediately over hot rice or noodles. Or to dehydrate, cool the ginger beef and broccoli and spread it on the dehydrator trays lined with fruit leather sheets. Dehydrate at 145°F for 12 hours until the broccoli is brittle and the beef is leathery and hard.

To Store

Dried ginger beef and broccoli stored in Mylar bags with oxygen absorbers will keep for up to 5 years.

To Rehydrate

In a medium saucepan, combine 1 cup of the Ginger Beef and Broccoli and 1 cup boiling water. Cover the saucepan and reconstitute for 15 minutes.

Hamburger Stew

Prep time: 20 minutes / **Cook time:** 40 minutes / **Dehydration time:** 12 hours / **Serves:** 4

Hamburger stew is a family weeknight favorite, with savory gravy and the rich flavor of aromatic vegetables. It is the ultimate comfort food!

1 pound lean ground beef

1 cup mushrooms, finely diced

4 potatoes, peeled and cut into ½-inch cubes

4 carrots, peeled and finely diced

2 celery stalks, finely diced

1 onion, finely diced

2 garlic cloves, minced

3 cups beef stock, divided

2 tablespoons tapioca starch

Salt

Freshly ground black pepper

1. In a large bowl, combine the ground beef and mushrooms. Form a large mound and let it sit for 10 minutes.

2. Meanwhile, in a saucepan, combine the potatoes, carrots, celery, onions, and garlic. Add 2 cups of beef stock and simmer over medium heat until the potatoes are soft, about 20 minutes.

3. In a skillet over medium heat, pour in the remaining 1 cup of beef stock. Add the beef and mushroom mixture to the skillet, breaking it up with a spoon into small, uniform pieces. Cook until the ground beef is browned, about 15 minutes. Stir in the tapioca starch and cook for 2 more minutes. Remove the skillet from the heat.

4. Add the cooked beef and mushroom mixture to the vegetables in the saucepan. Stir to combine well. Simmer for 5 minutes to blend the flavors. Season the stew with salt and pepper to taste.

5. Serve the stew immediately, or to dehydrate, spread the cooled stew on the dehydrator trays lined with fruit leather sheets. Dehydrate at 145°F for 12 hours until the carrots and potatoes are hard and the beef is leathery and brittle.

To Store

Dried Hamburger Stew stored in Mylar bags with oxygen absorbers will keep for up to 5 years.

To Rehydrate

In a medium saucepan, combine 1 cup of the stew and 1 cup boiling water. Cover the saucepan and reconstitute for 25 minutes.

Shepherd's Pie

Prep time: 35 minutes / **Cook time:** 1 hour / **Serves:** 4

This is my family's favorite recipe to use up leftover mashed potatoes and gravy. Traditional Shepherd's Pie uses lamb, but you can use any leftover meat for this recipe, or even mushrooms in place of meat for a vegetarian version.

4 potatoes, peeled

1 teaspoon sea salt

½ cup dried carrots (page 66)

½ cup dried onions (page 75)

½ cup dried peas (page 50)

½ cup dried corn (page 68)

4 cups beef stock

2 cups leftover cooked beef, lamb, turkey, or mushrooms

2 tablespoons tapioca starch

½ cup cold water

1 tablespoon butter

1. In a stockpot over medium heat, cover the potatoes with cold water. Add the salt. Simmer for 20 minutes, or until the potatoes are tender when pierced with a fork. Drain the pot and reserve the cooking water. Mash the potatoes, using a small amount of the cooking water to help them mash. Set the potatoes aside.

2. In a saucepan over medium heat, combine the carrots, onions, peas, and corn. Add the stock and bring to a boil. Remove from the heat and reconstitute, covered, for 20 minutes.

3. Preheat the oven to 325°F.

4. Chop the leftover cooked meat or mushrooms into bite-size pieces. Once the vegetables are softened, add the beef to the saucepan and simmer, uncovered, over medium heat.

5. In a small bowl, combine the tapioca starch with the water using a fork to fully combine. Pour the tapioca mixture into the vegetable-meat mixture. Stir consistently while adding to prevent lumps from forming.

6. In a shallow casserole dish, pour the vegetable-meat mixture. Spread the mashed potatoes over the top of the casserole. Top with the butter (it will melt while the casserole is baking, creating a brown crust on the potatoes).

7. Bake uncovered for 30 minutes, or until the casserole is bubbly and golden brown. Serve immediately.

Tuna Casserole

Prep time: 20 minutes / **Cook time:** 30 minutes / **Dehydration time:** 8 hours / **Serves:** 2

Tuna casserole is inexpensive and filling for a delicious budget meal. If you are avoiding wheat, gluten-free pasta works well in this recipe.

2 cups macaroni

2 tablespoons butter

½ onion, diced

2 celery stalks, diced

1 tablespoon tapioca starch

1 (7-ounce) can tuna, packed in water

1 cup chicken or vegetable broth

1 cup coarsely chopped broccoli

1 cup shredded cheddar cheese (for serving)

SERVE IT UP: For a kick of freshness, top the casserole with freshly chopped chives or parsley.

1. Cook the macaroni according to the package directions, but for a few minutes less so the pasta is al dente. Rinse it under cold water, drain, and set it aside.

2. In a large saucepan over medium heat, melt the butter and sauté the onions and celery until they are translucent and fragrant, about 10 minutes. Add the tapioca starch and stir it into the onion mixture.

3. Add the tuna and its liquid to the saucepan. Break the tuna up so it's in uniform pieces. Stir in the broth, and simmer over medium heat until the mixture begins to thicken. Stir in the broccoli and cook just until the broccoli changes color to bright green, about 3 minutes. Remove the pan from the heat.

4. Add the macaroni to the saucepan with the sauce. Stir the sauce to uniformly coat the macaroni.

5. Serve immediately with the shredded cheese sprinkled on top, or to dehydrate, arrange the tuna casserole in a thin and even layer on the dehydrator trays that are lined with fruit leather sheets. Dehydrate at 165°F for 8 hours, until the macaroni mixture is hard and brittle.

To Store

Dried Tuna Casserole stored in Mylar bags with oxygen absorbers will keep for up to 5 years.

To Rehydrate

In a medium saucepan, combine 1 cup of the casserole and 1 cup boiling water. Cover the saucepan and reconstitute for 15 minutes. Stir to mix the sauce with the macaroni.

Potatoes O'Brien

Prep time: 10 minutes / **Cook time:** 50 minutes / **Serves:** 4

Potatoes O'Brien are an interesting variation of hash brown potatoes. They are popular for breakfast and for a main meal side dish. Make them from dehydrated vegetables using broth for added flavor to reconstitute them before frying.

3 cups vegetable broth

2 cups dried potatoes, cubed (page 77)

½ cup dried sweet peppers (page 76)

½ cup dried onions (page 75)

2 tablespoons olive oil

1. In a saucepan over medium heat, heat the chicken broth until it bubbles. Remove from the heat.

2. Add the potatoes, sweet peppers, and onions to the pan. Cover and reconstitute for 20 minutes.

3. Stir the potato mixture and let it sit for 20 more minutes, or until it is fully rehydrated.

4. Heat a skillet over medium heat. Pour in the olive oil and heat for 1 to 2 minutes. Add the potato mixture. Brown in the oil for 5 minutes. Turn the potato mixture over and brown the other side for 5 minutes, or until the potatoes are golden brown.

ELEVATE YOUR DISH: Serve Potatoes O'Brien with fresh parsley and scallions, finely cut, and sprinkled over the top just before serving.

Peach Salsa

Prep time: 15 minutes, plus 1 hour to chill / **Dehydration time:** 15 hours
Yield: 1½ cups fresh = ½ cup dried

This fresh salsa recipe is best made with in-season peaches and tastes delicious alongside fish, seafood, or pork. Dry the salsa to enjoy its savory-sweet flavor with your winter meals.

2 ripe peaches

1 medium jalapeño pepper, seeded and diced

½ red onion, finely diced

2 cloves garlic, peeled and minced

¼ teaspoon sea salt

¼ teaspoon freshly ground black pepper

Juice and grated zest of 1 lime

2 tablespoons basil leaves, chopped

1. Wash the peaches in cold water to remove grime.

2. Blanch the peaches in boiling water for 1 minute to remove the fuzzy skin. Plunge in cold water to prevent the fruit from cooking. The skins should slip off easily. Cut the fruit in half and remove the pit. Cut the peaches into ¼-inch pieces.

3. In a medium bowl, combine the peaches, jalapeño pepper, onion, garlic, salt, pepper, lime juice and zest, and basil and mix to combine. Cover and chill for 1 hour to allow the flavors to meld. Serve immediately or dehydrate for later.

4. To dehydrate, arrange the salsa on the dehydrator trays lined with fruit leather sheets. Dehydrate at 135°F for 15 hours, stirring halfway through the time to encourage even drying.

To Store

Dried Peach Salsa stored in vacuum-sealed glass jars, protected from heat and light, will keep for up to 5 years.

To Rehydrate

In a large bowl, combine ½ cup dehydrated Peach Salsa and ¾ cup lime juice or water. Reconstitute at room temperature for 1 hour.

ELEVATE YOUR FOOD: Add ½ cup diced cherry tomatoes to the peach salsa for a more traditional salsa flavor.

Beef Stir-Fry with Soba Noodles

Prep time: 20 minutes / **Cook time:** 20 minutes / **Dehydration time:** 9 hours / **Serves:** 4

Colorful and hearty, this stir-fry features soba noodles, which add a chewy texture and nutty flavor. Soba noodles are made from buckwheat flour and wheat flour, lending additional fiber and protein to this dish.

1 (5-ounce) package of soba noodles

1 tablespoon toasted sesame oil, divided

8 ounces beef sirloin steak

½ medium onion, thinly sliced

2 garlic cloves, peeled and minced

1-inch piece fresh ginger, peeled and finely diced

1 hot pepper, cored, finely diced

1 tablespoon tamari

Juice and grated zest of 1 lime

½ cup carrots, peeled, cut into thin strips

½ cup red peppers, cored, cut into thin strips

2 cups baby spinach, washed

1. In a stockpot of boiling water, cook the soba noodles for 2 minutes, and drain. Toss with 1 teaspoon of the toasted sesame oil and set aside.

2. Slice the steak into ¼-inch slices. In a large skillet, heat the remaining oil over medium heat until it is sizzling. Add the steak and onion, and stir-fry them together until the meat is uniformly brown and the onions are translucent, about 10 minutes.

3. Add the garlic, ginger, hot pepper, tamari, and lime juice and zest to the skillet, and stir-fry for 1 minute. Add the carrots and peppers, and stir-fry until the carrots are tender-crisp. Add the washed baby spinach leaves and stir-fry just until the spinach leaves wilt, about 1 minute. Add the soba noodles to the skillet and stir briefly to coat the noodles with the sauce.

4. Serve immediately, or to dehydrate, place the beef stir-fry mixture and the soba noodles together on the dehydrator trays lined with fruit leather sheets. Dehydrate at 145°F for 9 hours or until the beef is leathery and hard.

To Store

Dried beef stir-fry stored in Mylar bags with oxygen absorbers will keep for up to 5 years.

To Rehydrate

In a medium saucepan, combine 1 cup of the dried stir-fry mixture and 1½ cups boiling water. Cover and reconstitute for 25 minutes. Before serving, gently stir to mix the sauce with the noodles.

MEASUREMENT CONVERSIONS

VOLUME EQUIVALENTS	U.S. STANDARD	U.S. STANDARD (OUNCES)	METRIC (APPROXIMATE)
LIQUID	2 tablespoons	1 fl. oz.	30 mL
	¼ cup	2 fl. oz.	60 mL
	½ cup	4 fl. oz.	120 mL
	1 cup	8 fl. oz.	240 mL
	1½ cups	12 fl. oz.	355 mL
	2 cups or 1 pint	16 fl. oz.	475 mL
	4 cups or 1 quart	32 fl. oz.	1 L
	1 gallon	128 fl. oz.	4 L
DRY	⅛ teaspoon	–	0.5 mL
	¼ teaspoon	–	1 mL
	½ teaspoon	–	2 mL
	¾ teaspoon	–	4 mL
	1 teaspoon	–	5 mL
	1 tablespoon	–	15 mL
	¼ cup	–	59 mL
	⅓ cup	–	79 mL
	½ cup	–	118 mL
	⅔ cup	–	156 mL
	¾ cup	–	177 mL
	1 cup	–	235 mL
	2 cups or 1 pint	–	475 mL
	3 cups	–	700 mL
	4 cups or 1 quart	–	1 L
	½ gallon	–	2 L
	1 gallon	–	4 L

OVEN TEMPERATURES

FAHRENHEIT	CELSIUS (APPROXIMATE)
250°F	120°C
300°F	150°C
325°F	165°C
350°F	180°C
375°F	190°C
400°F	200°C
425°F	220°C
450°F	230°C

WEIGHT EQUIVALENTS

U.S. STANDARD	METRIC (APPROXIMATE)
½ ounce	15 g
1 ounce	30 g
2 ounces	60 g
4 ounces	115 g
8 ounces	225 g
12 ounces	340 g
16 ounces or 1 pound	455 g

RESOURCES

FoodSaver

FoodSaver manufactures food preservation vacuum systems and accessories for vacuum-sealing dehydrated food, including accessories to seal Mason jars. FoodSaver.com

LEM Products

LEM is an American manufacturer of dehydrators and accessories, including plastic screen material rolls that can be cut to fit your dehydrator. LEM also carries jerky spice blends, vacuum sealers and bags, canning jar vacuum-sealer attachments, and oxygen absorbers. LEMProducts.com

PackFreshUSA

PackFreshUSA specializes in American-made Mylar bags, vacuum bags, and oxygen absorbers for packaging dehydrated food for storage. PackFreshUSA.com

Visit JoybileeFarm.com/DehydratorCookbook for bonus dehydrator recipes.

INDEX

Acknowledgments

The writing of this book was a more joyful task because of my editor, Sierra Machado, who kept the vision of the book in focus and encouraged me through the writing milestones.

My husband, Robin, was a rock, taking care of little jobs like laundry and dog walking so that I could focus on the tasks of writing and recipe testing. He willingly ate up the dehydrator experiments so that I could get the recipes right. When a weather disaster took out the main highways in British Columbia, and the grocery store shelves were bare, with just two weeks until the manuscript was due, he willingly drove around looking for one more bag of onions and potatoes so that I could keep testing recipes for the book.

My daughter, Sarah Kirchhevel, created four months of fresh content for the Joybilee Farm blog so that I could focus on writing and recipe testing.

About the Author

 **Chris Dalziel** is the founder of the popular websites JoybileeFarm.com and TheDIYHerbal.com. Chris empowers her readers to grow their own food and preserve it so that they can confidently provide for their families. She is a teacher, author, gardener, herbalist, and homesteader. Chris believes in giving her readers a quick win, because each quick win builds confidence and empowers self-reliance. Chris and her husband live in British Columbia with their three dogs and three cats.

CPSIA information can be obtained
at www.ICGtesting.com
Printed in the USA
JSHW030919290822
29767JS00001B/2